H u n t e r s
Beware

You are the prey and you are endangered!!

By George

A collection of short stories about the experience and wisdom gained by 60 years of hunting and fishing

authorHOUSE

1663 LIBERTY DRIVE, SUITE 200
BLOOMINGTON, INDIANA 47403
(800) 839-8640
www.authorhouse.com

First published by AuthorHouse 07/13/04

ISBN: 1-4184-5579-2 (e)
ISBN: 1-4184-3077-3 (sc)

Library of Congress Control Number: 2004092955

Printed in the United States of America
Bloomington, Indiana

This book is printed on acid-free paper.

OMEN TO THE ANIMAL ABUSERS

You went to the forest to hide your face,

The animals cried out no hiding place,

The animals cried out we're burning too,

We want to go to heaven same as you,

No hiding place down there.

Purpose of this Book

To alert the hunter of old, that great male provider and protector of the family, that he is endangered and is on the way down and out and he is being replaced by a better hunter.

To alert the modern sport hunter that he too is endangered. He is being voted out by ridiculous laws that say no hunting allowed which really means no guns allowed, and that poisons and foolish laws will replace him and his gun as a weapon of choice to control the animals.

To alert the general public of the giant GENDER ROLE REVERSAL that has already started and will soon reach it's sweeping climax with complete FEMALE DOMINANCE - - bringing TEARS OF JOY TO THE WOMEN and TEARS OF WOE TO THE MEN. - - It's only a few generations away.

Table of Contents

Personal Goal of the Author

To prove the old hunter and fishing adage. "God doesn't count the time spent in hunting and fishing, when calculating a man's allotted time on earth. Since he spent 60 years hunting and fishing and since the average life span is 71 or so the author should live a ripe 131 years. The author is now 81, that which would give him another 50 years, unless he fishes and hunts some more. Then it could be longer. Let's wait and see.

About the Author and His Beliefs

George is just an average guy who was drawn to hunting and fishing at an early age of 10 or 11 years. It was an unexplainable urge but a very definite lure to these hobbies. The experiences in this book are an attempt to answer the question of why men hunt. After an early introduction to the sport, George used this newly gained knowledge to increase his earning power working as a sales manager for a small abattoir (slaughter house) located in

Washington D.C. and later to further his own research biological supply and exotic food business (World Safari Inc). He was just an average hunter who was never a good marksman. He was not a gun fancier he had only the necessities and was a pretty fair fisherman. He was also pretty good at finding animals that were considered exotic at that time. A series of circumstances lead George into an interesting way of earning a living. Hopefully any young readers (young hunters to be) might learn from these experiences and avoid making the same mistakes. The older hunters might enjoy these experiences because they themselves have had similar experiences and can relate to the author. Fortunately George had the ability to predict trends and demands because his income depended upon it. He was instrumental in introducing many natural and often exotic foods to the diverse ethnic culture of the international community in the nation's capital and elsewhere in the country. Some of the exotic foods included buffalo, deer, wild boar, wild sheep, lion, land antelope, quail and quail eggs, rattlesnakes, lizards, emus, ostriches, pheasants, turtles, wild hare, frogs, alligators, crawfish and bear. The underlining theme for this demand can be summed up in a brief but true statement, one mans trash is another man's treasure. At no time is this book meant to be a scientific journal or a "how to do" hunter's manual. It is just an easy to read history of a participant who enjoyed the fruits and benefits that automatically accrue to men in a male dominated society that lasted for 1 million years and is now changing rapidly to a female dominated one. I'm hoping that the book will alert you that you are an endangered species and you are the prey. Your role as the primary hunter and provider is fast coming to an end. There is little or no hope for you because you can't compete. Like the dinosaur you will become extinct.

An Introduction

For the purpose of the book fishing will be dealt with as hunting since they are the same. The reasons people fish are the same as reasons people hunt, only the prey is different, as its habitat is water. The equipment used to harvest them is different also; rods, reels, lures, and nets instead of guns and decoys. While most so called gun hunters fish not all so called fishermen hunt. When a group of so called fishermen are asked, "Do you hunt?" Some will answer, "I don't like guns, I couldn't take a gun and shoot a pheasant or a rabbit, but I like to fish." "But sir," I would respond, "you are a hunter; you seek out the prey (fish), lure it in close, subdue it, kill it and hopefully eat it." Admit it, we are all hunters and we do it because we like it. When hunters are asked, "Why do you hunt?" They usually reply, "I don't know why I hunt but I know I like it", then after a brief pause they will begin listing reasons for leaving a nice warm bed at the break of dawn and often face cold weather and discomfort to satisfy their primeval urge to survive and bring home meat for the table, clothing and protection. Some of the reasons given are;

1. I like the taste of wild meat: This is a good excuse to go hunting, but is not a good reason to hunt. You can buy better tasting farm raised game at the meat market. Sometimes wild meat does taste good but more often than not it doesn't. Wild meat can be tough, stringy and tasteless, usually because the housewife who has to prepare the game has had little experience in cooking meat that is often lean and tough. But don't blame her, you're the one who brought home the tough old buck or the goose that had been flying back and forth from Canada for the past 15 years. For guaranteed good eating bring home a tender young doe or the small goose that was flying at the end of the formation. It is probably his first flight and he is

still tender. The old ones are out in front breaking the air currents for the youngsters in the rear. They are the tough ones.

2   The "Macho man" excuse: To prove his masculinity in a sophisticated world. This is an attempt to prove his ability to protect his family and maintain his standing in a society which no longer needs physically strong protectors. He hunts for trophies to hang on the wall and has pictures of game in his wallet, usually taken when he was a young hunter or fisherman. I know this because my den wall is full of trophies and photos.

3   The camaraderie excuse: This is a rapidly growing excuse to hunt. Men like to join with others with the same interest. They get together to drink, tell stories, joke and make fun of one another and other manly things. Very often this means getting away from it all, the pressures of

the demanding or boring job, bad boss, nagging wife or just to recharge the old batteries.

4 The "Big Brother" excuse: "An older brother or father was a hunter so I became one." Getting started in hunting very often is a learning experience and we copy others. That is how I got started.

5 Love of Nature: These people like to get out in the woods and observe the animals and hunt with a camera and, if fishing, they release the catch. They pick the occasional wild mushrooms, huckleberries and herbs. This is a good reason.

6 I like to kill: This is a poor reason to hunt, but it is there. Rarely will a man admit it, but some do. This type becomes very apparent when you are in a hunting situation like a duck blind or any shooting situation. They will shoot first, shoot at anything that moves and shoot at

game out of season. True hunters shun and avoid this type of personality. He is an explosive type, releasing pent up frustration and anger in the only way and place he is able to. He certainly cannot do this at his home or in his work environment. This is a poor excuse to hunt.

7 Customer relations: Many firms use hunting and fishing as a form of entertainment to further their business aims. Nothing softens a customer or a potential client like an expense paid hunting /fishing trip. It worked well for me. Since hunters have a difficult time explaining their reasons for going hunting just imagine how hard it is for the non-hunter to understand why he does it.

In the beginning God created all living things. On the 6th day He created man and said "Bear rule over the animals of the earth, the birds of the air and the fishes of the sea." With this admonishment man's dominion over the animals of the land, birds of the air and fishes of the sea was established and is in effect to this day and cannot be changed. <u>It is God's Law</u>. In plain words man can do what he wills with all the living creatures. He can hunt them for food, use them for work, keep them for pets and yes even use them for research.

On the sixth day God created man and said "Bear rule over the animals, birds of the air and fish of the sea.

This is God's law and cannot be changed.

You can hunt and eat them, put them to work, tame and pet them and you can even use them for research.

The author says that if you abuse them you will lose them.

When early man and woman looked out from their cave and saw all these goodies man said to woman "I have the bigger body, muscles and bigger heart to pump more blood through my bigger lungs so I can run faster, I will be <u>The Hunter</u>," he says, "and since you are built for child bearing and nurturing of children, picking of berries and fruit you will stay close to the cave and take care of the children and keep a nice warm, clean cave and cook the meat I bring to the table." Thus, the roles of the male as hunter and female as homemaker were established and exist to this day. However, since this is a *man-made rule,* it may be changed and is being changed now. This worked well for more than a million years because the male hunter fulfilled his role of bringing food to the table, shelter and clothing, as well as protection for the family. With the millennium (2000 AD) came the gloom spreaders who were predicting the end of the world. They were mistaken, but the year 2000 AD might very well be the beginning of the end of the role of the male as the hunter and female as homemaker.

As society progressed, man learned to contain and farm his animals. Later the male hunter became even more efficient, he got a job, earned money, and hunts at the supermarket and brings home meat for the table; he shelters and protects his family thereby fulfilling his role of male hunter. He may be called by different names, such as, plumber, carpenter, lawyer, or mason, and even though he goes about it in a different way he is still satisfying his primeval urge to feed, clothe and protect his family. Regardless of what you call him, he is the male hunter of old. Even if we change his name, he is still the male provider and protector of the family.

The modern or the recreational hunter goes forth laden with equipment, subdues a few animals, but doesn't fulfill any of the criteria of the male hunter of old. He brings little or no food for the table and doesn't provide food or shelter for the family. He isn't protecting his family from wild predators, his hunting is all recreational, just a symbol of what it was, it is now all fun and games.

There are two hunters: the hunter of old (the real hunter and provider) and the modern hunter (all recreation).

Let's deal with the evolution of the old hunter first. (See if you can find any resemblance to the hunter of old and the modern hunter or better yet the hunter in you, in these experiences.)

As society progressed from a hunter and gatherer to one that farmed and contained animals (ranches), the hunter of old becomes more efficient and gets a job, earns money and hunts his meat at the supermarket. While this new method of providing for his family was easier and more efficient it began opening doors for a new and better hunter to enter the scene.

Hail the rise of a new hunter. The door opened wider during World War II when many of the male hunters had gone to war. Women began entering the work force for the first time in great numbers. They got jobs doing the work of the male, getting paid money, shopping at the supermarket, bringing food for the table. Women realized they were able to do it as well as a male hunter.

The realization of this new opportunity brought a release from the woman's role of the past million years.

With the introduction of female contraceptives like the pill ---even greater freedom was now available. She may still carry the burden of child bearing and child nurturing, but she can now decide when she will have the children or maybe not even have them at all.

This new development places the role of the female hunter on an even level of that of a male hunter. The future roll of the female hunter grows ever stronger while the role of the male hunter diminishes. The female hunter is stronger and more capable in this changing environment. This is readily apparent from insurance statistics. Women live longer than men. There isn't much need for the male hunter, big body, large muscles, and big lungs in the modern world of technology, even wars will become mere push button affairs. Opponents will not even see each other. Unmanned aircraft, space vehicles, laser weapons etc., will deliver destruction thousands of miles away with a push of a button by either male or female. With the increasing equality of the sexes, the roles of the male and the female are being shared equally and in some cases reversed and will be dealt with later in this book but for now lets us examine the modern day hunter and the role he plays in today's society.

George Gets Hooked

This is a series of experiences depicting the evolution of a modern day hunter from a neophyte to an aged conservationist.

The beginning of this journey starts in a small mining town in central Pennsylvania in 1935 when George, a young boy of 11 has the urge to fish. He does not know why but he has the urge. An older neighbor has him digging worms (night crawlers) for him and promises one day that George could go fishing with him. He can't wait for that great day. Finally, Sly, as the older boy is called, said "today's the day, get ready; you get the worms, we leave at 3pm and I'll pick you up." Now that was a great honor for the young boy since Sly was the local man-about-town. He was the pitcher on the baseball team, the best shot at the pigeon shoot, he was handsome, had a car and many girl friends. The country was just coming out of the depression and few people had cars, but Sly had one. He showed up and had George get in the back with his worms. George observed the equipment in the back with him and he understands the hooks, the sinker and the lines, but he doesn't understand why Sly brought the blanket and the girl. They arrived at the river. Sly baited the hooks and flung the line into the water. He had no rod, only a lines, sinkers, bait and hooks. He threw the one end with the baited hook and sinker into the water and attached the other end of the line to a screw bell device, a simple metal screw with a spring on top and a bell attached to that. The whole apparatus is about 8 inches long and when the catfish bite it would jingle the bell (this was especially helpful when it became dark) the bell would alert the fisherman that he had a catch. He would pull the fish in and take it off the hook and put the fish in a wet burlap bag. He would then bait the hook again and throw it back in the river. He had about 12 of these lines going at once. He showed George how to manage the whole procedure and then goes and sits by the fire with the girl. After a few jingles, George catches on fast and is able to handle the operation including how to take the catfish off the hook without getting stung by the spines. Sly had a very efficient operation which kept George very busy running up and down the river answering the jingles and catching the fish. Not paying attention to Sly and the girl. Occasionally he could hear noises from the blanket on the other side of the fire. George caught on to the mechanics of fishing rapidly but at 11 years of age he couldn't quite grasp what was going on under the blanket. I guess the reasons for fishing that night was catching fish (food for the table) and camaraderie. It wasn't just the fish that got hooked that night. George was hooked on fishing for life.

George's Introduction to Hunting

Fall of the same year his older brother Big John was going rabbit hunting. George wanted to go along but didn't know why. He just wanted to go (underlining the primeval urge to bring meat to the table) or he just wanted to learn from Big Brother. Big John said, "OK", and off they went to the hills owned by the mining companies that surrounded the town. Big John carried the only equipment they had, an old single barreled shot gun. George would walk the low ground beating the bushes and brush trying to scare up a rabbit for Big John to shoot. This was not too successful as they shot only one rabbit for the whole season. This wasn't too bad considering how few rabbits were to be found around the abandoned coal mines, how many hunters there were and how little equipment they had. (This was during the depression after all).

But things were about to change for the brothers. Big John got two jobs, one at the mill during the week and one up town on the weekends. He bought a new pump gun and new hunting jacket which had a pocket in the back to carry the game he would shoot this season. With his new hat, calf high boots and fancy britches that fit into the boots, he was the cat's meow, as they used to say, a sight to behold. Big John was ready, the only thing now needed was a dog to flush out the rabbits and so he went to the next town to buy one.

He got "Rover", a hound that was everything a rabbit hound should not be; he was big and fast, too fast for rabbits. What he really needed was a small beagle hound that trailed the rabbit by scent slowly letting out a howl every so often, letting you know where he and the rabbit were. The rabbit is so much faster than the dog that he will often just move ahead of the dog, often stopping to listen for the dog and giving the hunter an easy shot.

The rabbit often comes back to the same spot from which he was flushed again giving the hunter an easy shot. But hunting rabbits with Rover was nothing like that because he was too fast. It was Thanksgiving Day, the last day of the small game season. It had been a miserable season with very little game and we were determined to bring home the bacon and the glory that goes with being a successful hunter in a small mining town. So off we went, Big John in his new outfit, pump gun, Rover and George, with no gun, tagging along. George was too young to get a license. After trekking the hills for half the day without seeing a rabbit they were about to give up when, lo and behold, there went a rabbit and there went Rover and there went Big John after them. Bang! Bang! Bang! George rushed over to Big John "Did you get him?" asked George. "No! Darn it" replied Big John and as he was reloading his gun here came the rabbit again with Rover right on top of it. They ran right by us. Bang! Bang! Bang! Went Big

John's gun again. "Did you get him?" asked George again and again and Big John replies "No! Darn it, I missed him because he was going too fast and I was afraid to shoot the dog." Big John reloaded again, and we could tell by the barking of the dog that the rabbit had holed up.

George raced to the scene, which was nothing but two large slabs of rock lying horizontally with a small space between. Lying on his side, he could see the rabbit. Big John joined the scene and, what a scene it was! Big John put down his gun and was bent over George asking "Can you see him?" "I can reach him," replied George. And all this time, Rover was going crazy, digging at the rocks. Big John asked George if he could get the rabbit. "I'll try," he said as he reached in, grabbing the rabbit by the hind legs attempting to pull it out. Not knowing much about rabbits he wasn't sure that they wouldn't bite. The rabbit began scratching furiously and George let go of it. The rabbit and Rover dash right between Big John's legs who then picked up his gun and shot.. Bang! Bang! Bang!. George asked for the third time "Did you get him?" "No! Darn it. I missed again" replied Big John. Just then Rover was barking and the rabbit was holed up again. This time they walked to where the rabbit is holed up while the dog was digging furiously. Big John then leashed the dog and dragged it away from the hole saying, "enough is enough, that rabbit deserves to live after all it has been through." And then, "Let's go home."

On the way down the mountain Big John told him several reasons men hunt but all George could think about was how he wished they'd gotten the rabbit because it was Thanksgiving Day and it could have been a nice dinner (food for the table) if they had. He was practically in tears as he complained how he had the rabbit in his hands and let him get away. Big John told him, "It wasn't your fault it was mine, I missed him nine times.

But all that is not important" said Big John.

We had a nice time together (camaraderie reason), we enjoyed

the fresh air and being out in the woods and we met a nice rabbit

(love of nature). George learned a lot from this day. He learned

that rabbits don't bite they scratch, Big John was fair when he

said; "the rabbit won the right to live another day," and that Big

John was awfully bowlegged as was proven when the rabbit and

the dog ran through his legs.

Hear the Rabbit Cry

I heard the rabbit cry... George is a little older now and he went rabbit hunting with a group of friends and while separated from them saw and shot a rabbit. The rabbit was not dead, but its back was broken, and with its front half erect it was trying to drag its lower back and hind legs along but they won't go. And the rabbit was crying, a sad mournful cry, somewhat like a baby but not quite. This cry devastated George and as if this wasn't enough he had to dispatch the rabbit by hand. This affected George since he so loves his own dogs and cats so much. When he arrived home he tried to make a proud entrance and holding the rabbit by the hind legs, he entered the kitchen where his mother and pregnant sister are preparing dinner. His sister took one look and screamed, "our George is a murderer," and she ran crying from the house. This second bout of crying is almost too much for George as he wanted to cry too but boys in coal-mining don't cry. George's hunter's virginity was lost and by hearing the rabbit cry, a youthful exuberance was lost and by hearing the sister cry the desire to hunt rabbits is gone. He vows never to shoot another rabbit again and he never does.

This experience curtails his desire to hunt anything for some time. He often wondered how many hunters have heard the rabbit cry, probably not too many as rabbits usually die outright when shot with a shotgun. If they did hear a rabbit cry many would stop hunting rabbits. This split between loving some animals while enjoying hunting and shooting others is a very difficult dichotomy to understand for both the hunter and the non-hunter. Maybe that is why most old hunters become wild life conservationists. They end up feeding the birds contributing to programs such as, save the pandas, the wolves, bears, ducks and whales. Old hunters never die they just mellow with age and become conservationists. I have often wondered if it is true that

God doesn't count the time we spend hunting and fishing when

he determines our life span.

Lost in the Wild

Hunting and fishing can also be used as a tool to further business with old clients and to solicit new business. Since hunting has become so expensive many firms use it as a form of entertainment to further their business and solicit new business. Nothing softens a customer as an all expense paid hunting or fishing trip. George discovered this excellent tool while working as sales manager for a small firm in the nation's capital.

An important customer asked George to join them on a hunting trip and his employer insisted he go (what a tough assignment, an all expense paid hunting trip. This, to George who was having a tough time making ends meet (hunting is very expensive for hunters who live in the city) was a dream trip, requiring transportation to far away hunting grounds, lodging, food and equipment. Fundamentally, it was a trip of camaraderie, i. e., playing cards, eating, telling jokes, making fun of one another all while sleeping in a nice warm farm house, with a housekeeper who had hot food ready when ever you wanted it and also some hunting. He learned from this trip that hunting and fishing trips are excellent ways to promote business and are considered legitimate business expenses, but customer hunting is like playing customer golf or squash, you let the customer win. In hunting you let the customer shoot first and get the game and go home with the trophy and see that this is done safely. George, when he acquired his own exotic food business followed this rule faithfully.

He leased farm land on the eastern shore of Maryland and hired guides, dogs and even at one time rented an island. This promotion was a success. All the customers were meat buyers from supermarkets and restaurants and many were from other countries such as France and Italy and some were even well known. They enjoyed hunting in the USA very much. They said that only the wealthy could afford to hunt in Europe because of

the shortage of hunting grounds.

Here are some experiences George had with his clients:

Customer Hunting or Lost in the Wild

The result of the deer hunting trips with customers evidently pleased George's employer because he insisted that he go with them when ever they invited him. This was fine with George because the trips were an all expense paid hunting trip on company time, but one trip had a few surprises. He was going deer hunting with bow and arrow but he had no bow hunting experience. In fact, coming from a small mining town he had no archery experience at all. But George rose to the occasion and ran out and bought a bow, arrows and even a quiver, a bag for the arrows with a strap to place over your back. The merchant who sold him the bow must have known that he knew nothing of the sport because he sold him a 60 pound pull bow (wanting to get rid of a hard to sell item). 35 or 45 pound pull is plenty strong enough for a deer. When he joined the hunting party he was the butt of the jokes like, who is going to help you pull, TARZAN???

Or, we are hunting deer not buffalo. Nevertheless they decided to go straight up the mountain, dropping off each hunter about 100 yards apart.

They put George down farthest up the mountain.

The plan was to sweep the face of the mountain and regroup later for lunch. Because they had a housekeeper cooking for them and it sounded like a safe, and easy hunt, George got permission to bring his 9 year old son along who would stay at the farmhouse with the housekeeper until they returned about noon. But things were about to change this day. No sooner did the other hunters leave George to begin their sweep to flush out the deer when the fog began to rush in. Within minutes George couldn't see 10 feet in front of him. The terrain changed also, with big rocks to climb over and crawl around. Needing both hands free he dismantled his bow, slung it over his back and placed the arrows in the quiver. He kept moving in the direction he thought was the meeting place, yelling in an attempt contact with the other hunters but there were no answering calls. After a while he realized that he was out of hearing distance and the fog is getting even worse. To add insult to injury a slight drizzle has started. He just keep moving in the direction he thought was the meeting place, calling out every once in a while but still no answer.

Several hours later his stomach was growling so he determined it must be about noon. He finally gave in to the fact that he was lost. The rain was seeping through his water repellant jacket which he thought it was waterproof. Trying to find an opening in the big rocks, he crawled around hoping to find some shelter from the rain but to no avail. It must have been about 8 hours that he was up there without seeing or hearing neither a living soul not even an animal. He realized he must get out of the weather before night fall even though it looked like night already. He finally came across a stream and decided to follow it downhill.

It must join a larger stream or run into a lake with habitation

somewhere. But being thirsty after the long walk he laid on his

stomach to scoop up handfuls of water into his mouth. Just then

he raised his head and saw a deer on the other side of the creek

which was only about 10 feet wide. The deer had lowered his

head as if it was going to take a drink too. They stared at each

other in disbelief. The deer seemed to be observing this strange

creature stretched out on his stomach drinking like an animal.

The very animal he came to hunt was right in front of him but

he never gave thought of trying to shoot the deer, he was just

happy to see another living creature. The deer faded into the

fog and George got to his feet and felt relieved for some reason.

Maybe it was the deer that gave him encouragement or maybe it

was just the drink of water that lifted his spirits but with finding

the stream. His hopes soared. He decided to follow the stream down hill, sure that it would run into something good. And sure enough, after walking for another 2 hours he came to a small farm at the foot of the mountain near the town of Toms Brook. He met some locals who listened to his predicament and agreed to drive him back to the farmhouse were he was supposed to be. They arrived just as a search party was getting ready to go out for a second attempt to find him. The first attempt was cut short because of the fog. George had never been happier especially to see his son who must have been worried when his father didn't return with all the other hunters. George was very fortunate to get off that mountain alive. He didn't even have matches and those mountains get awfully cold at night.

He realized how fortunate he was when the very next weekend a scout master and his troop were caught in the very same area in a snow storm. The troop stayed together and was taken out safely but the scout leader perished. What George learned from this experience is to never hunt alone if you can avoid it. Keep

in touch with your friends or group. Always carry a compass.

Weather such as fog and snow can obliterate landmarks. Always

carry matches in a small waterproof container which he did for

the next 20 years. Luckily he never had to use them. Dressing

appropriately in rain gear and -warm clothes is important. And

always expect the unexpected to happen. No one expects to get

lost, but it happens.

About George and His Partners

Lest anyone believe the author is an avid hunting freak, nothing could be further from the truth. He loved going hunting, loved the outdoors, and loved most of the fellow hunters, but he was not fond of all the people he hunted with, nor with all aspects of hunting.

He hated cleaning the guns, cleaning the game, and caring for the fishing equipment, but fortunately he had Pappy and Rudy. They took care of everything, including him and the clients. He was a spoiled gentleman hunter. Maybe not quiet a gentleman, just a spoiled hunter. Not even a good hunter. What started out as a youthful sport became a part of his lifestyle and a substantial part of his income.

Pappy was a retired police officer and a gunnery officer who taught police recruits gun safety and shooting. He was a marksman of great skill, having many national awards for pistol shooting, and he loved shooting and cleaning guns. George never cleaned a gun or the game in 25 years of hunting with Pappy.

Rudy loved to take the guests out when George wasn't available. He was a tough boxer in his own country and was in training with the hope of getting a fight with Joe Louis when WW2 broke out. Twenty-five years later, Rudy who claimed to be afraid of no man, confessed one day, after having met Joe

Louis and Rocky Graziano when they visited our meat processing

plant, that he wasn't sure he could have beaten Joe Louis. After

being introduced to Joe and shaking hands with him he took

George aside and said, "Did you feel how strong his arm still is?"

Evidently boxers can gauge the strength of their opponents by

several methods and arm strength is one of the ways. Not being

a boxer I can't prove or disprove this but knowing Rudy, this was

one hell of a confession to make.

Rudy, Pappy, Joe, Rocky, George, and our broker Sidney

went out that evening. Everyone had liquor but Joe who had

ginger ale. Maybe there is a lesson to be learned here, that not

drinking or drinking ginger ale may keep you as strong as Joe

Louis. Drinking and hunting are not a good mix, especially

with strangers. The reason for mentioning the valuable qualities

of Pappy and Rudy is because hunting with strangers can be

dangerous. When Pappy said " don't ever point a gun at a man unless you intend to kill him," you listened and when Rudy told you to sit down, you sat down and obeyed.

The Mouse that Bagged the Hunter

While hunting pheasants on a farm in Pennsylvania with Jock, who had a famous family restaurant in Virginia, George received a call that required his being present at a business meeting one hour away. He decided that Pappy would take the party out while he drove to the meeting. However, the guests insisted that he hunt with them for an hour or so, and then he could go to the meeting. He agreed although he was wearing only street clothes. He took his place in the line of hunters and was on the end closest to the road. Pheasant hunters always line up to work a field, not only is this an efficient way to hunt upland game but it is also safest because everyone knows where every one else is while the dog goes in front searching for the pheasants. When the dog scents the bird, he comes to a standstill pointing to the location of the bird and waits for the order to flush out the pheasant. It was about 10 o'clock on a nice warm October day. Wearing street clothes and waiting for the signal to start, he shifted his foot and felt a sharp scratching that shot rapidly up his left leg, under his jockey shorts and still scratching. He grabbed the left cheek on his back side and grabbed whatever was doing the scratching with his left hand and still waving the shot gun in the right hand, he yelled for help. Pappy came to his aid. He put down his gun and kneeling, he unbuttoned George's belt and pants and reached into his shorts and pulled out a mouse. Imagine how fast it happened, in the matter of seconds, the mouse was up George's leg and under his shorts. He wondered where the mouse was going so fast and what was his final destination? Of course there were a lot of wise remarks like, "Are you going to have it mounted?", or, "It's probably a girl mouse and she likes you," or "You were very brave to have held your ground when that fierce mouse charged", etc. He found out that day why hunting pants are tight around the ankles and why it is important if you are going to hunt to wear hunting clothes. Not like Jean Louis who owned a French restaurant at the Watergate in Washington, D.C. He decided to meet George, Pappy and Rudy at the duck blind on Maryland's Eastern Shore. We gave him directions on how to get there and told him to dress warmly as it would be cold. Sure enough Jean arrived on time but he had parked about 100 yards from the blind. There was about 15 inches of snow on the ground with about an inch of ice crusting the top. He tried to join the group. With each step he would go crashing thru the ice crusted snow. He soon discovered that his fancy French boots and his fancy trendy leather jacket were no match for the rough weather that often goes with duck and goose hunting. Sadly, we helped a shivering and shaking Jean back to his car and sent him home because he was really cold and suffering from exposure. He never got to the duck blind. The lesson learned from this experience is that if you're going hunting, dress accordingly and as the host you must make sure your guests get home safely. This

is of primary importance.

The Shortest Hunting Trip Ever

While hosting a client from Baltimore, George learned that hunting was not the same for all hunters and the game they were after was not the same. He and Rudy were to meet a client at a shore duck blind (a wooden structure covered with brush) on the eastern shore of Maryland. They gave the client, Andy, directions to the blind and he was going to meet them there at daybreak. It was a glorious bluebird day while they waited. Finally, Andy arrived around noon. He pulled up to the blind in his Cadillac with a blond in the passenger seat. He got out of the car wearing a suit and top coat with a hat and tie as though he were going to a business meeting. He walked the few steps into the blind with a bottle of whiskey in his left hand and his gun in his right. He stood right in between Rudy and George and looking out the side of the blind where Rudy was he said to him, "I don't see any ducks, do you Rudy?" Rudy replied, "No, not now". Then he looked out George's side of the blind and said, "I don't see any ducks, do you George?" and George replies, "No, not right now." He then turned and walked away, leaving his bottle of whiskey and said, "When the ducks arrive call me; I'll be down at the motel."

The whole episode lasted less then a minute which made it the shortest hunting trip ever ----it probably was a very successful trip for the client since he was married. Let's hope he didn't exceed the legal limits—for game in possession.

The Most Pleasurable Hunting Trip

Hunting is often a tough physical experience on rough weather with rain, sleet or snow. George is always concerned about the safety of his clients. A trip with Jock, a noted restaurateur from Great Falls, Virginia, was different. He was always pleasant, witty and entertaining. Imagine you are in a goose blind, which is nothing but a hole in the ground about five feet deep, with a little bench to sit on, in the middle of a harvested corn field, with no creature comforts, cold and wet, and worse yet, the geese are not flying. Things are pretty miserable at this point and almost like magic Jock presents us with steaming hot steaks, French rolls, wine, desert and even linen napkins. He was a gentleman in every way and *this* day hunting was not about work and no play. Pappy and George just relaxed and enjoyed themselves because they didn't have to worry about gun safety with Jock.

Wild Boar Hunting

Is it really wild boar? Is it really hunting?

A client had seen a magazine ad for wild boar hunting in the mountains of Tennessee and wanted to go. George wanted to accommodate him and agreed to go. They hopped on a plane, flew to Tennessee, rented a car and drove to the hunting camp to spend the night at the lodge. They had a nice meal and sat around talking to other hunters who were going to hunt in the morning also.

Hunters are an interesting lot for many reasons. To begin with they come from all walks of life and some have saved their money for quite a while just to make this trip. Others like the man who flew in on his private plane, kept shining his gun while displaying his pictures of the Kodiak bear he had shot. It was a big bear alright and so was his gun. He was constantly showing everyone what a great gun he had. He most certainly was a gun fanatic. A large gun would be appropriate for shooting a large bear, but a little brush gun was good enough for wild boar, but to each his own. Anyway we went to bed that night and got up the next morning to have a nice breakfast. We hopped into a jeep with a guide with two dogs running alongside as we drove a short distance to the top of a hill and dropped off each hunter about 100 yards apart. The guide took the dogs into the brush and soon the dogs are barking and howling , chasing after the wild boars that they located. The boars run by you and of course you shoot at them. This is not much of a hunt as the boar is supposedly wild but he doesn't seem to be. The two dogs, one small and one big get the boars moving. The big dog, running much faster than the little dog, corners the boar and actually tries to bring it down on his own. The boar will always beat the dog one on one since the dog has no good place to grab and hold and if he tires or gets careless or loses his footing in the struggle he will then be slashed by the tusks of the boar. That is where the small dog comes in. The small dog bites the boar about the ankle of his back leg causing the boar to turn to attack the small dog, giving the big dog another chance to try to pull the boar down. When the boar again turns on the big dog, the little dog bites his back leg again. It must hurt the boar badly because he turns on the little dog which is quickly dodging out of harms way giving the big dog a chance to seize it again. This goes on until the boar decides to run away from his tormentors and seeks a better spot to defend himself. The boar finds a good spot to stop running giving the hunter a chance to catch up and get close enough for a good shot.

About the boar: He probably was of wild boar stock but most likely had been farm raised. When the hunters arrive they bring out one boar per hunter and release them to be hunted. This is really a simulated hunting experience that preserves the animals and is more of an orchestrated event with a guaranteed result. It

is not a bad experience for someone who has only a short amount

of time and the money to pay for it. The expense is eased when

you bring home your catch of 250 to 300 pounds of meat, which

is some of the best pork you ever had. Really!!!

Customer Hunting – Caught in the Act

Customer golf is like tennis, handball, squash or any other activity in which you lose in order to make your client feel good toward you and the product you are trying to promote and sell. George used this tactic to his advantage time after time with great results. However, the best laid plans often go astray.

When entertaining an experienced hunter we would let him shoot first. However, when entertaining an inexperienced hunter, Pappy and George would shoot at the same time as the client, there being no way the guest would know who really shot the goose. They would immediately turn to the guest and slap him on the back and say, "Great shot, you got your trophy". Now the guest is not sure who shot the goose but since being patted on the back and he really wants to bring home some game to show is friends and sons he begins to think that he might have shot the goose. This worked fine until one day when a client discovered our little scheme. When caught up in the moment Pappy and George didn't realize that the client hadn't even shot his gun. When we started slapping him on the back and saying what a great shot he made, he responded, "It must have been a really great shot because I never ever raised my gun." Yes, the best laid plans often go astray.

As Good As It Gets

The exotic food business is not all work and no play. Here is an encounter to prove it. While calling on the chef in the Watergate complex, I was greeted by the chef who took me to the bar and treated me to a drink while conducting our business of providing him with exotic food and game. Seated at ea nearby table were three very distinguished and well dressed women. They had just returned from attending a play at the Kennedy Center. One was about thirty five and the one was forty five and the third was fifty five. I was very flattered when they invited me to their table and even treated me to a drink. After the drink, they invited me to join them at a birthday celebration dinner at a fashionable restaurant in Georgetown in Washington DC.

Since women don't usually treat me to dinner and drinks I was very happy to accept the invitation. The dinner was to be held the next day at a very nice restaurant which was also a very good customer of mine. I thought that mixing business with pleasure

was as good as it gets. The restaurant owner was present and

greeted me warmly and sent complimentary wine to our table. It

was a very enjoyable event. But I knew there was no such thing

a free ride.

I thanked the ladies and preceded to leave when one of them

took me by one arm, slowing me down, as another took the other

are and strongly insisting that I accompany them. Being single at

the time I didn't struggle too much and in fact was flattered and

wondering where they were taking me. Making sure I wouldn't

escape they marched me directly across the street to private club

in a hotel. The ladies were apparently members because they

had ID card to get into the club. I was dressed in a nice suit

and tie and the club was hot and with perspiring dancers on the

dance floor. One of the ladies took me to the dance floor to dance

with her. When we were through dancing we walked over to

where the other two ladies were sitting and the next lady got up immediately and took me to the dance floor. After dancing to a couple of songs we returned to the other ladies and again and the third lady stood up and drug me to the dance floor. I never even got a sip of my drink.

By this time my clothes were a mess and my tie was undone. I was so wet with sweat that it felt like I was wearing a wet blanket. I'm tired and confused. I can't remember ever having been wined and dined by three attractive women. I was wondering which of the three ladies I was going to spend the evening with. They danced me until I was dead on my feet and covered with perspiration. It was like dancing with a jack in the box. Now sooner had I got back to the seat when another fresh and rested dancer popped up ready to dance. After tow or three hours the dance was over, I was no longer thinking of romance,

I only wanted to go home and rest. They drove me to my car, dumped me off and drove off laughing.

After resting a moment I started my car, leaned back and rehashed the evening's events. I realized the ladies were not attracted by my charming personality; they only needed a dancing partner for the evening. With that realization I too laughed. It was a lot of nice clean fun at the expense of an ordinary man who thought he might be a Clark Gable type for a short time. I mention it only to show that I could supply more that just exotic foods.

The Ladies apparently enjoyed the evening and the games they played with me. They sent me and invitation to join them at another party two weeds later but unfortunately, I had to decline as I had to go out of town to catch rattlesnakes in Texas.

Hunting without Guns

George and Rudy were hosting a hunt for a big client and his administrative assistant, Bob. It turned out to be an interesting hunt. First of all the buyer himself was unique because he was the only Mormon with whom George ever hunted. He was a very gentle, kind, soft spoken and non swearing man and his buddy was the exact opposite. He was robust, outspoken, forceful, confident and willing to take on just about anything. George hunted with them several times and reflecting back he remembered that Mike never shot anything. His buddy Bob on the other hand did all the shooting on the trips. Mike conveniently was always doing something else when the opportunity to shoot arose and Bob was always there and ready. Mike seemed to enjoy going hunting and enduring the cold and discomfort. He also enjoyed bringing and preparing food for lunch. He always had a fire going and cooking something. On this particular day they started on their way home from the eastern shore after hunting ducks all day.

They had to cross the Chesapeake Bay Bridge on the way home

having been hunting about 10 miles on the other side. Rudy

and George got in their car and Mike and Bob got in their own

vehicle. It was getting dark as they start toward the bridge which

is the easiest way home from where they were hunting. George

left about 5 minutes after the guests. After driving about 5 miles

toward the bridge, George noticed that Mike has pulled over on

the side of the road, his lights were on, and the doors and trunk

of the car were wide open. George pulled over behind them just

as they were dragging a deer toward their car putting it in the

trunk. The car was a Volkswagen so the trunk was in the front

of the car. George asks what happened, thinking they were in an

accident and hit the deer. They were out of breath, showing signs

of exertion and were disheveled when George approached them.

They explained to George what had happened and how they just had a wrestling match with the deer.

As they were driving down the highway the deer ran across in front of them without getting hit by a car but it stopped on the side of the road on a grassy knoll. It apparently was exhausted and looked as if it was about to fall over. So they pulled over and Bob got out of the car and tackled the deer. The deer started to fight and Bob wrapped his arms and legs around the deer to hold it down. He then called to Mike to get something to knock the deer out. Mike went to the trunk and got the tire iron to hit the deer. Mike being the gentle, kind man that he was refused to hit the deer. He said he was afraid of hitting Bob but George believed he didn't want to hurt the deer. Bob was getting tired and irritated with Mike and told him to grab the deer and he would hit him. So they changed places and now Mike is the one wrestling with the deer. Bob picked up the tire iron and struck the deer to kill it and load it in the trunk. That's when George showed up. Relieved that they were not hurt or in an accident they all got back into their cars and proceeded down the highway. Suddenly, like something out of a gangster movie, there came a thumping and banging from their trunk. Mike and Bob pulled over followed by George in time to see Bob open the trunk begin hitting the deer again. After subduing the deer they went through the bridge tollbooth and headed their separate ways. George learned you don't always need a gun to get your deer.

The company that Mike worked for had a wild game dinner annually and the deer would be served. George was invited but declined. He didn't find it appetizing to eat a deer that was killed with a tire iron. He wondered what others at the dinner would think if they knew.

The Most Considerate Hunter

When hunting with his two brothers, Pauly and Pasqual, in a goose pit on the eastern shore of Maryland, George was enjoying the first flight of the geese to come and together they shot three. Later a second larger flight came in with enough for everyone. After a lot of shooting, the George noticed that Pasqual was just sitting there while everyone else was shooting. They asked him why didn't shoot. "You didn't even raise your gun," He replied that he was letting his brother have a chance because he hadn't shot a goose yet and he was waiting till he got one, then he would shoot again. This surprised us because so many of the other hunters were committing offences, such as shooting before the geese were in range. Pappy and George were used to letting the clients shoot first but this was the first time they ever heard of another hunter waiting for someone else to get a chance at a goose. It's usually a difficult thing for a hunter to refrain from shooting when the geese are swirling all around him

and he has been waiting all day for a shot. Acts of kindness and

consideration do often happen on a goose hunting trip.

The Wonderful Female Kidney

The question was, would she and if so *where*? While entertaining another of our French chefs we ran into a interesting problem. The guest's safety and comfort were always uppermost in our minds. The client had brought along a young girl friend. This in itself was not the problem because we often had guests with their wives or girlfriends along. But this time we were in a goose pit which, of course, had no powder room. Usually there are facilities in walking distance, such as a farm house. But this time we were far away from any such comfort. The goose pit, as described earlier, is a 5 foot deep rectangular hole in the middle of a huge cleared corn field. There was no place to hide. Modesty is not a problem for a party of men.

We all met at 5am at a restaurant catering to hunters. We had a nice big breakfast and coffee because we would be out in the goose pit all day. At the guest's request, we ordered lunches and coffee to go, in thermoses. We were driven to the middle of the corn field and made arrangements to be picked back up at 5pm, the legal time to stop hunting for the day. As the day progressed some of the men began to climb out of the pit and relieve themselves. No one, not even the boy friend, had noticed or even considered that the poor girl had not gone nor did she have a place to relieve herself. After shooting for a couple of hours, the men began taking turns relieving them again. By this time Pappy noticed that the poor girl had not gone to the bathroom since they left early that morning. The client was having a great time and the shooting was great but he was oblivious to the poor girl friend's suffering and it looked as though he was never going to want to leave. After 9 hours Pappy suggested that we go because he was feeling sorry for the girl but the client was stubborn and wanted to stay for another shot. Finally at 5pm the driver showed up and we left. The girl ran into the restaurant in a hurry while

Pappy and George got into their car to head home. As usual, we discussed the trip and how it went but this time we commented on the amazing bladder the poor young girl must have had and how inconsiderate the client was to her. We never did like doing business with that man and now we had more proof of what an arrogant bum he was. We decided we would never take him on a hunting trip again.

George asked Pappy if he ever noticed that when ever they'd take out a bad client the client's bad habits got worse and when you'd take out a nice client they'd act nicer, like our friend Jock. This selfish arrogant client and this poor girl with the fabulous bladder married but were divorced shortly after. No need to wonder why.

The Ivy League Hunters

A bluebird day is a name duck and goose hunters give to a warm balmy day with no wind nor clouds, just blue skies. It's a day when the game birds are not flying; they just sit on the water out of gun range resting. They seem to be enjoying the respite in their daily search for food and like the hunters seem to be enjoying the nice weather. On this unexpectedly warm day in the middle of winter, George and his friends found themselves removing their outer warm winter coats and hats and even opening their warm woolen shirts to stretch out in the brush of the hedge where they were hiding. Ordinarily they would use the natural brush and hedgerow for cover when hiding from the geese as they flew overhead. The geese would hear their calls as they lured them to come down and join their decoys. This day the birds were not flying, they sat on the water, resting and soaking up the sun, George and the guys decided to do the same, lying in the nice warm weeds to take a nap after they had their lunch. The birds did not fly that day so they just rested, unsuspecting that they were lying in either poison ivy or poison sumac and would be heading to their family doctors for relief from the horrible itching before the day was out.

George went to the doctor with an unusual winter ailment. His face, eyes, hands and even his male member was swollen like a fat sausage. He asks the doctor what it was and the doctor says that it's herbal, that's for sure. He was surprised because it is winter. The doctor told him that he could get it at any time; however you normally get in spring or summer but that he really got into a good crop and must have been rolling in the stuff. It was about December 15th and the doctor informed him that he might get rid of it in time for Christmas.

The lesson learned from this hunting trip is to expect the unexpected.

Canadian Fair Play

George was invited on a ten day fishing trip to Canada by three of his best customers who he also considered friends. He decided to join them because they showed him a 48 inch great northern pike that was in their freezer. He had never caught a great northern and was excited to try. They began the journey by auto as far as they could and then flew to their final destination. The last stop, before the flight into the interior was a rustic bar and eatery. They drank some beer and George bought a bag of potato chips, which was a mistake because they later made him ill. After a beer or two he asked the owner where the restrooms were. He directed him to the door and told him he'd have to go outside because the plumbing wouldn't thaw out till June and here it was only May. So he went outside and was surprised when a couple of Indian women (squaws) walked by without even giving him a second glance. This amused him because he was not used to coed, community, all outdoors, bathroom facilities.

So they finally left to head out fishing on a nice sized lake in the middle of nowhere with a couple of primitive huts. They made bets on who would catch the biggest fish and George vowed that he would not shave until he caught a great northern pike.. He did end up catching one thirty six inches long. They took a picture of it and while he was holding it up for the camera it broke loose from the chain by shear force and bent the big safety pin latch which was pushed through its jaw and fastened like a very large safety pin. With one shrug he broke loose and took off. It was fortunate that others witnessed it or George would still be wearing a beard.

While we were enjoying our fishing a guest joined us. He was a member of the Canadian Parliament and he stopped by to say hello to the rest of the group who were friends of his.

George didn't know much about the man beyond his political status but he did learn about his health. He was a diabetic. He was big and heavy and it upset George when he saw him insert a needle into his abdomen until the others told him it was just insulin shot for his diabetes. He learned about his unbiased social views first hand because he kept asking George, "Why do you Americans treat your black people so badly." This took George aback and he replied the he didn't treat anyone badly. He got alone with George again and again asking him the same question. In the meantime George was feeling sick from the bad potato chips. Coupled with the politician's constant carping about the American's treatment of the black people, George is becoming irritable. Since he has to keep replying that he didn't treat anyone badly he concluded that the man is seeking some wisdom from him, or just trying to make him feel bad or trying to paint all Americans with the same brush. Even though he is upset he tries not to show his annoyance.

The day before they were to leave, a seaplane landed with a man and woman and their Indian guide. The man and woman came ashore and joined the group for introductions and drinks, leaving the Indian guide to unload their luggage. After a few drinks we walked them to their little hut, where they came upon a strange spectacle. The Indian guide who had unloaded their luggage was out cold, drunk and sprawled all over the luggage with an empty liquor bottle on the ground. He was sprawled in such a grotesque manner, that we thought he was dead. Just then the Canadian politician who kept asking "Why do you Americans treat your blacks so badly," came upon the scene and began to rant and rave about how all the Red SOB's are drunken bums and how you can't trust them near a bottle of whiskey and how they are all the same. "You can not trust a single one." This is what

George learned from this trip. Don't buy old potato chips from a bar out in the boondocks. That bathroom plumbing doesn't thaw out until June in some parts of Canada. Great northern pike have very strong jaws. And some biased Canadians, like some biased Americans, misjudge people by holding a whole group responsible for the actions of a few.

Stay Away From My Girls

Rudy and George were going duck and goose hunting hunt for the day at a farm on the eastern shore of Maryland. They arrived early in the morning when it was still dark. Rudy had been driving while George got in a few extra winks. On arrival at the farm, Rudy got out of the car first and went to knock on the farmer's door. George got out of the passenger's side and removed his heavy padded hunting coat from the back seat. After the car's lights went off there was complete darkness. He had just finished buttoning up his jacket and was standing all alone when he was dealt a mighty blow to the mid section. It drove him back against the car and he slid to the ground. He pulled himself together and tried to get up when here it comes again, another hard blow to the mid section. This time he was driven back against the car and down to the ground again. This is all going on in complete darkness and to say the least he was confused. He tried to get to his feet again and then considered staying down and taking an eight count when he was saved by Rudy and the farmer. The farmer was wielding a big stick and Rudy was running around yelling. George wasn't sure what was going on because of the darkness and he thought that maybe they were at the wrong farm and that the farmer had taken a stick to Rudy. He could hear the farmer cursing at someone. Finally some light was shone on the situation when the farmer's wife opened the kitchen door. Very apologetically, the farmer explained that the SOB did this all the time and as dawn broke, George got to see his attacker. There, silhouetted on a little rise of ground, would you believe it, was a ram surrounded by his harem. As it turned out that he was defending them. The farmer explained that he would like to take the ram to the slaughter house but his wife wouldn't let him. When asked why he didn't give him to someone else the, the farmer told them that he would give them all to someone who would give them a good home but no one would take them because the ram was so mean. Rudy had just bought a farm and agreed to take them. The next day he sent a truck for them. Since then Rudy has passed on to a better hunting ground and so has the mean ram but Rudy's offspring are taking care of the Ram's offspring to this day on Rudy's farm in Louisa, Virginia. It's a strange world.

Gentle Milton

Milton was a frustrated, failed writer, so he said' but George

never believed it. George thought he was very good but just gave

it up to get a job to pay the bills. He was a frozen food buyer for

a food distribution company. Not a very imposing figure sitting

behind a big desk, he wore glasses, was short and a bit round.

In addition, he was just recovering from a heart attack and an operation to remove one lung.

They had a good business relationship and later they became good personal friends, but at this time it was just a business relationship. George was very surprised when Milton took him into his confidence and told him about a personal problem he was having. He said he would like to teach his two young teenage boys how to fish but he didn't know how. He'd heard George telling others that he knew something about fishing and would appreciate it if he would teach him. Because he was a customer George said OK.

He took Milton to the Potomac River which was nearby and started him with worms but soon progressed to the Rappahannock where they floated and waded with inner tubes harnessed to their bodies and began casting for bass. He later took Milton to the Shenandoah where he taught him how to catch hellgrammites and use them for bass bait, and then on to the Saint Johns River in Florida where they were mentioned in the local papers for their excellent catch. In Lake Wales, Florida, they caught a large mouth bass that still hangs on the wall of George's den. They say Field and Stream Magazine would give you honorable mention if you caught a bass over 10 pounds. This fish was over 10 pounds but was never recorded. At Lake Okeechobee their outboard motor conked out and they were faced with the possibility of spending the night with the awful mosquitoes, gnats and the occasional roar of a bull alligator announcing his need and desires. Another group towed them out

In the Chesapeake Bay, George's 14 foot fiber glass boat sank and they floated for about an hour before they were pulled from the water. Thank goodness for the life jackets, they made all the difference in the world. Without them an unpleasant incident could have very easily turned into a disaster. The Washington

Post newspaper reported the incident in the sports section which

went something like this, "Local sportsmen float in water and are

passed by fishing boats on the way to the fishing grounds." This

was true but we were in choppy water which made it hard to spot

us. We were sure that if they saw us they would have picked us

up.

George and Milton progressed to deep sea fishing off Ocean

City, Maryland, anywhere from 30 to 80 miles out to sea seeking

White Marlin. George also has one of those hanging in his den

where every once in a while he will look at it because it brings

back memories of better fishing days. Milton would also go on

to catch a Mako Shark which was later classified as a game fish.

He is now a more imposing figure, seemingly bigger, and the

desk has grown smaller. He wants to go deer hunting and asked

George if he would take him. George is taken aback as this is

a problem. A good friend, with a bad heart and a missing lung wants to go deer hunting in an area where there is a lot if uphill mountainous walking while carrying a heavy gun. He knows how much it would mean to Milton, just to be able to say he is going deer hunting, it would make his chest swell. So George agreed and they met at a farm house in the Shenandoah Valley at daybreak. The regular hunters share this farm house with a cook and all the usual creature comforts.

The farm was at the foot of the mountain with a little pond about 50 yards from the house. It consisted of open fields with little brush and a few trees for about 200 yards at which point the woods began beyond the pond. A shallow ditch ran through the field. George had surprised a deer or more correctly was surprised by a deer there the previous year after hunting on the mountain all day. With all the hunting that day George ended up getting his deer only 50 yards from the farm house.

Milton arrived exactly at dawn with a shot gun he had

borrowed. George waited until all the hunters had gone up the

mountain then led Milton to the pond and positioned him next

to a fence post and told him not to leave or even move around.

He told him that he knew he would feel silly by being close to

the farm house but the deer were down in the valley where they

have been feeding all night and would be trying to get back

up the mountain to sleep and avoid all the daylight noise and

commotion. Milton looked confused but agreed to stay. George

proceeds up the mountain and stayed for a couple hours, then

decided to check on Milton. He found him exactly where he told

him to stay. He was excited so George asks him, "What's up?"

He blurted out that he thought he shot one. "What do you mean

you think you shot one?" he asked him. "I saw a deer and I shot at

it and it went down right over there." "Well is he dead?" George

asked Milton. "I don't know, " he replied and pointed where the deer went down by a little hill. He asked Milton, "Why didn't you look and see if he is dead?" He told George, "I didn't go to take a look because you told me not to leave this spot." So they took a look and sure enough, there over a little rise was a dead deer. They took the deer into town to have it checked and tagged at the check station, and he told Milton, "let's go back to the farm house and have lunch," but Milton was anxious to get home to show everybody his deer. George understood after all, how many men get their deer the first time they go hunting and with their first and only shot?

Riding back to the farm house, George couldn't help thinking about that proud man going home with his deer and how much taller he would look behind his desk. George was proud of himself; because he had made a hunter out of the man in one day.

Snakes, will they or will they not?

The question is, will snakes attack an artificial lure, and if they do would it be for food or only to defend themselves? That was one of the questions George tried to answer on this particular fishing trip. My friend and fishing partner Milton was a frozen food buyer. Through his work with the frozen food producers he was treated to an all expense paid fishing trip to Lake Wales, Florida. Milton was allowed to bring a guest and invited George to go along. This trip included a fishing guide who knew the area well. When they assembled the next morning at the dock they met the guide and took off in his outboard. George thought this guide was rather strange, being about 60 years of age and he mumbled to himself constantly. With the motor running you couldn't tell what he was saying but George knew that he would not have been his first choice as a guide. But the trip was free so who was he to complain. When they got out in the middle of the lake the guide shut off the motor and they got their tackle ready to fish. George noticed that the guide was preparing to fish too which is not uncommon. Some see that their clients get to the fishing grounds and help them find the fish but this guide was going to fish right along with them. That was still fine with them and when he opened his tackle box, he had a little pistol in it. George asked jokingly, "Why do you have a gun, are we going to shoot the fish?" Very seriously he replied "I shoot the snakes, every one that I see, don't like them, they scare the hell out of me and I hate them and they hate me." He showed them the pistol and the little bullets he used. George had never seen a small caliber gun that fired little brass bullets loaded with many tiny pellets just like a shotgun shell. He knew several people who were deathly afraid of snakes but who would believe that a guide who makes his living on lakes and rivers would be so terrified of snakes. He tried to tell George the snakes smell our food and come close to us because of the odor. George didn't believe this

at all. He tried to tell him so, but the guide became very agitated,

so he just let's the subject drop and started to fish.

The fishing was fair and they caught a few, but the guide

didn't catch any and you could hear him mumbling to himself.

To make matters worse, George latched on to a really large bass.

He reeled the fish in and it proved to be well over ten pounds.

The guide was so upset, ranting and raving. He had been fishing

50 years and had never caught a bass over 10 pounds and these

dumb guys came down from the city and in one day they got

caught a big one. George believed he said catching a bass over

10 pounds gets a mention in a sports magazine if you record it

but George never recorded it. You would think the guide would

be proud that one of his guests caught a trophy like this fish but

not this guide. He continued mumbling and saying not so nice

things about George. He was not going to get George's vote

for best guide of the year that's for sure. After he caught such a nice fish George thought he would stop fishing and give the others a better chance to latch onto some big fish and catch up to him. Hopefully this would reduce some of the tension that was building up in the little boat. He pulled out a sandwich and began to eat his lunch. Lo and behold, a snake surfaced about 30 yards away. The grumbling guide is trying to say "I told you so," but George knew the snake didn't smell the sandwich and chips, or the beer. He was sure it was a mere coincidence, but he has his own agenda. He was wondering if a snake would strike at an artificial lure if it was presented properly. With a silver spoon lure still attached to his line he thought this would be the perfect time to test his theory. He planned to cast the lure about five feet beyond the snake and pull it right by his head to see if it would strike at the spoon and result in a catch. This would prove that snakes would react to lures and be caught with this method. However, he made a few mistakes that day. First his cast was short and the lure landed close to the snake's head. He instantly pulled back on his rod and the snake was hooked. From that distance he couldn't tell if the hook is in the mouth or he just snagged him, so he tried to bring it in for a closer look. He is beginning to reel him in when he realized his second mistake. He is in a boat, in the middle of a lake; with two men who are deathly afraid of snakes and one of them has a bad heart. While George was reeling in the snake the two men are screaming and swearing and both were scrambling to the front of the boat trying to get far away from the snake. He reeled the snake in right along side the boat and reached for the net which wasn't anywhere near him and realized that it's foolish to ask two screaming men to hand it to him because they are busy yelling obscenities at him. With the snake along side the boat, George still can't see where the hook is attached because the snake is all wrapped up in a ball. He took his rod in his left hand and grabbed an oar in the other and tried to slowly unravel the snake to see where the hook was imbedded. This brings more yells and curses from the men who were afraid that he was going to flip the snake into the boat. He was pushing on the snake with the oar which released it.. It drifted away from the boat and quickly dove out of sight. His question was never answered. Would a snake attack an artificial lure? He did however have his answer from that fear ridden, snake hating guide, who immediately cranked up the boat and announced, muttering, "Were going in." It was only about 10am and all this happened in about three hours.

Except for the guide mumbling under his breath, nothing more was said until we got to the dock. Poor Milton was quiet and exhausted by the time the event was over but the guide had some choice words for George once the boat was unloaded, referring to George's sanity, his birth right and expressed a strong desire to never to see him again.

We took the big fish to a taxidermist to have it mounted and it's on George's den wall to this day. They left Lake Wales and went to Lake Okeechobee to fish the next day and George never got the answer to the snake question and if any one else knows it please contact him a <u>georgem@metronets.com</u>.

What about the Learning Experience

George had leased an island on the eastern shore of Maryland to entertain his clients with duck and goose hunting excursions. The Little Island was just that, a little spit of land about 2 acres in area and about one half-mile from the mainland which required an outboard motor boat to ferry the clients back and forth. Ordinarily, this worked fine until one evening when he and Rudy were taking the clients, with their equipment and their game, back to the mainland. Rudy said he would help the guests to their car and get them on their way while George secured the boat.

This was usually a two man job, wherein George would take off the motor and hand it to Rudy who would then hoist it up on the dock. That's the way it was supposed to work and usually did, but Rudy was dawdling with the guests so he decided to do it by himself. Because he was wearing hip high rubber waders he got out of the boat and into the water which was only about three and a half feet deep. He unscrewed the clamps that held the motor to the back of the boat and attempted to put the motor on the dock. It was too heavy and it slipped from his grasp and it fell into the water with George still holding on. It pulled him forward face down toward the water. Instantly, the cold water zapped him in his unprotected mid-section which was covered only by a cloth shirt which is no protection in the cold water. Paralyzed and motionless just bent over with his face only inches above the water he stayed that way until Rudy came back from seeing the guests off. He was close enough to the dock so that Rudy was able to pull him upright and out of the water. What he learned from this experience was that cold water is dangerous and can paralyze and that no hunter should ever hunt alone especially in or on the water where the unexpected can and does happen.

Saddest Day of Hunting Ever

George, Rudy and Pappy were scheduled to take some clients out to Little Island for some goose and duck hunting a couple of days after George's incident in the cold water. Rudy was to get the blind ready for their guests which consisted primarily of putting out about 40 decoys. George was to come a little later with the guests.

As Rudy was loading the boat for the trip to the island an uninvited friend named Johnny showed up and asked if he could join him for a couple hours of hunting. He had a gun he had borrowed from another friend; the gun was a family heirloom. Rudy noticed that he was very upset and distraught and even though Johnny was not a client, Rudy allowed him go with him for a couple of hours. The weather was taking a turn for the worst but a little bad weather is usually good for hunting ducks and geese. The weather was becoming consistently worse and was getting too bad to continue the trip so George cancelled it and sent the guests home. He believed Rudy was alone on the island not knowing about the uninvited friend who had joined him.

Knowing that a little outboard motorboat would not be able to bring him back safely, George got the owner of a larger boat to take him to the island. While on the way to the island the weather became even worse, going from bad to ungodly in a very short time. The Chesapeake Bay is known for fast rising storms and the next day the locals would say this was the worse they had ever seen. The big boat took George to the island but had difficulty getting close enough to unload him. Finally, after several attempts the boat owner managed to get close but he was afraid of running aground and ruining his boat. He found a sandy spot and George dropped off the bow and scrambled up the shore. The boat owner said he couldn't stay any longer because it endangered his craft but he would come and get them as soon as the storm died down. George located Rudy, who was waving his arms and pointing to the water, and shouting, 'Johnny, Johnny, Johnny." George looked very carefully but he couldn't see Johnny. The boat was visible and didn't seem to be moving, it was upturned. He couldn't tell how long Johnny had been out there because Rudy was so upset. What torture he must have gone through knowing a friend was in trouble and not being able to help. The overturned boat was the only boat on the island. Johnny had shot a duck and had taken the boat to retrieve the bird and the boat had overturned in the rough sea.

A large fishing boat was passing the island on its way to shore with other hunters who had to come in from another island further out because of the bad storm. George walked into the water as far as his waders would protect him. He waved and shouted to the boat to no avail. In desperation he fired his gun in their direction, got their attention, and they came to pick them up. He immediately told them what had happened to Johnny. They circled the island and found the overturned boat but no sign of Johnny, so they took us ashore to notify the bay authorities. Because of the storm and impending darkness they would have to wait for first light to search for him. George and Rudy joined the Bay Authorities at dawn and they found Johnny on the first sweep of the area. His rigid body was placed on the boat in a horizontal position. His arms were stretched skyward and his hands were clenched. The authorities said he probably was clinging on to the boat which was the right thing to do since the boat would eventually wash to shore. Unfortunately the anchor had fallen from the boat when it overturned was dragging on the bottom which prevented the boat from getting close to shore and Johnny lost consciousness due to the cold water.

Someone mentioned that three other hunters were rescued that same day when their boat had overturned. Luckily, they were close to the shore when they became paralyzed by the cold water and were unable to move. The authorities said Johnny did not drown but died of exposure. They learned later, after his funeral, that the reason Johnny was distraught was that his divorce would be finalized that day so he borrowed a gun from a friend and went hunting. Perhaps he thought a successful hunting trip might help to relieve his distress. Maybe his distress caused him to be less careful in a dangerous environment. Strangely enough the heirloom gun he had borrowed was still in the boat, wedged under the seat. This tragic event shook everyone including friends and clients so much that we decided that hunting with many different people was dangerous enough but going to and from an island by boat was just adding to the danger. They never took a party to the island to hunt again.   Lesson learned, cold water can paralyze

and cold water can kill.

Farmer Teaches the City Boy about Living Well in the Country

George was living in the city in Northern Virginia next door to a retired farmer, named Fry, who still maintained his farm homestead in the Shenandoah Valley. Although he was considerably older than George they developed a friendship that lasted for many years with many pleasant memories but also had some surprises.

One weekend Fry invited George to spend a couple days at his farm to do a little fishing. This was great because Fry had a housekeeper to cook for them while they were fishing. He had also invited a young friend who knew the river well and who fished all the time so he knew where the best fishing spots were. At three in the afternoon they arrived at the river to meet the young fisherman who brought along a bottle of bourbon. Of course they joined the young man for a drink, then another and another all the while fishing and catching bass. At nightfall they divide their catch and parted ways with their young fishing partner. On their way back to his farm, Fry decided to stop by his neighbor's farm to introduce him to George. They pulled into a pitch dark farm yard and George wondered how Fry can just show up unannounced at someone's house. Of course, there are no cell phones or any other way to let the farmer know he has company dropping in at night, but George discovered that some means of communication withstand the test of time. Fry gathered up some small stones and began throwing them at an upstairs window. You would expect that he might break a window because he had little too much bourbon. Too hard a throw or too big a stone and crash goes the window. But nevertheless the farm communication system worked well because the lights went on all over the yard. Then a huge man appeared in the window standing in his white underwear with a pistol in his hand

and a gun belt strapped to his waist asking what the hell were

we are doing in his yard? Fry says waving a bottle of bourbon,

"it's me you old SOB, I want you to come down and meet a

friend of mine and have a drink with us." By this time George

is having doubts about meeting a big irate gun slinging farmer

who had just been roused from a nice comfortable bed, but Fry

is insistent and when the kitchen door opened George decides to

chance it. After exchanging greetings, the farmer sat them down

at a large table and they all took a nip from the bottle. George

notices the big man is sort of observing him almost as though

he is making up his mind about something and trying to decide

what to do with them. Then it seemed like he made a decision

and was zeroing in on George. The talk somehow got around

to liquor and George mentioned Benedictine Brandy, or B&B,

as it is commonly known. The farmer reached down under his

sink and brought out a bottle of B&B and gave George a sip and left the opened bottle on the table. The talk went on and on and the subject of rice wine was brought up. This time the farmer reached into his cabinet and brought out a bottle of rice wine. He gave George a sip and he left this bottle on the table. Next Haig & Haig scotch was mentioned and lo and behold the farmer again reached into the cabinet again and brought forth a bottle of Haig & Haig giving George a sip and again leaving the bottle on the table. Of course, the next subject is gin, and guesses what? That farmer repeated the process bringing out a bottle of gin, giving George a sip and leaving the bottle on the table for the forth time. How long they sat there or how many different drinks he had, George could no longer be sure, but he later realized that Fry only had a sip or two and the big farmer had nothing after the first drink from the bottle of bourbon.

Fry's housekeeper, who became concerned about them because they did not return from fishing, was out looking for them. She saw the light in the big farmer's house and decided

to get help to find them. There she found them and somehow

got them to Fry's place. She later told them that the table was

covered with opened bottles and that Fry was in very bad shape

but George was in worse shape by far. They had to put him to

bed because he couldn't make it on his own. It must have been

a child's bed because it was awfully tight quarters, built into the

wall in the unfinished back of the old farm house. When George

awoke the next day, about noon, he. looked up on an unfinished

wooden roof and discovered he was fully clothed, even with his

shoes and hat on and his hands folded nicely across his chest. He

was in a tight unfinished wooden box-like container. A terrible

thought flashed through his mind, "George you really did it this

time," he thought to himself, "you are dead in a coffin, about to

be buried." Just then he wiggled his toes inside his boots and

because they moved George went further and tried to get out of the little bed. Being successful he walked through the house, out the door, into his car and drove off for home. Those who saw him leave said that he raced out of there as if the devil himself was after him. Maybe he was. The lessons learned from this fishing trip are: drinking and fishing are not a good combination; bad things can and do happen; and some farmers are a lot more sophisticated when it comes to food and drink than we think. Especially this big farmer, he was flying live lobsters into his farm in the boondocks 20 years before the city sophisticates were aware of their availability. City boys can learn a lot from farm boys, this one taught me not to mix my drinks, not to drink too much and not to throw stones at a big smart farmer's window in the middle of the night.

Unexplained Incident or What Was It?

The summer of 1950 found George and Pappy fishing in Lake Seneca, trolling for steelhead trout. Some fishermen think this trout is really salmon that never went to sea. They may be right but I could never prove or disprove it. Lake Seneca is one of the five Finger Lakes in upstate New York. It is 25 miles long and about 400 feet deep, cold lake with a rocky bottom. While trolling along in a small outboard motor boat in the middle of the lake, they stopped to eat their sandwiches. It was about two in the afternoon on a beautiful sunny day, not a ripple on the water when right before their eyes something appeared in the water. It came right up to the surface of the water without breaking it. The thing seemed to be observing them from about ten yards away. They were awe struck and didn't move or say a word. It wasn't menacing and it stayed only a minute or so and then disappeared the same way it came, which was unusual in itself. It went straight down, not turning in the slightest and without causing as much as a ripple on the surface of the water. Most fish would propel themselves with their fins and tail. This did nothing!!! It just went down and from what we could see it had no dorsal fin. From what George and Pappy could see it had no fins at all, not even a tail! The best they could describe it from what they saw was that the front end was that it was three feet in diameter like a barrel and the color seemed to be a shade of brown. They tried to explain it away by imagining it was a barrel but that didn't work. If it was a barrel it would have broken the surface like most barrels and it wouldn't have descended as it did, it would have to have displaced air to enable it to submerge or create a ripple in the water or something, anything! There is no way this could have been an inanimate object. It was a live creature. It didn't look like a fish, at least no fish George had ever seen. In fact, it didn't behave or swim like any fish he had ever seen. It just seemed to ascend and descend with no fish like motions. Years later, when they would meet, the first words out of their mouths were, "Do you remember that fish thing we saw at Lake Seneca?" And the reply would be, "Do I remember it? How could I forget?" I know that many who read this would assume that they had good imaginations or too much to drink but regardless, this is what they saw, this was and still is an unexplained sighting. If anyone reading this has had a similar experience in Lake Seneca please let the author know. This has been bothering him for many years and if it can be explained he would like to put it to rest.

Bear Hunting or Barely Hunting

Bear hunting is a specialized sport with a very small number of hunters, an elite sport for which you need very little equipment. There are specialized dogs that can track the bears, run all day and fight against a tough opponent such as a bear to keep him cornered until the hunter arrives. This is no small effort since the bear is often large and is equipped with a tough protective hide and powerful claws that can rip a dog to shreds in a matter of minutes. The dogs must have great endurance since the chase and struggle may go on all day or until the hunter catches up to him and the prey. Since this is in the mountains, it can be a long time before the hunter gets there and it's sometimes into the next day. There is no time for stopping for chow, just running and fighting. Since this is a small elite group, George was flattered when he and Rudy were invited to participate in a bear hunt. They drove thru the night with no sleep and met with the dog's owner on a mountain road in Southwestern Virginia. There was a slight drizzle that day and after a brief introduction, they had an opportunity to examine the dogs.

They were big. One was an African ridge hound and the other was black and tan and looked like a huge hound. George had always been interested in dogs. After petting them for a while, he grabbed the hide of one of the dogs on the shoulder with his left hand and the top of the loin area with his right hand and stretched upward about six inches of skin. It was as though someone was wearing a suit several sizes too large. The dog's owner pointed out that the season was nearly over and that they run off a lot of fat from running all day and by the end of the season there is no fat left. We started up the mountain and immediately realized that this was not going to be an easy hunt. The dogs practically dragged them up the hill. It was a good thing George had a sling on his gun because it enabled him to put it over his shoulder leaving both hands free to hold onto the dogs. They were very strong and very eager to get on with the hunt. We could have used a couple more hands. The group of dogs that were ahead of them had picked up a scent and were off and running and George's dogs, eager to join the hunt, dragged him to his knees before he was able to unleash them. Rudy had already freed his dogs and they were eager to join the others. We thought the other dogs had already cornered a bear and that we could catch up to them and get ourselves a bear. We slipped –slid down into the hollow over rocks, slid on wet leaves, with brush hitting us in the face for about a quarter mile from the action. We thought we had it made, but no such luck. The action went further up the hollow then stopped again. We tried to join in the fray again but as we got near the bear is on the move again. This time the action is up hill and again stopped. We continue scrambling to catch up, but at a slower pace. The action seemed to settle down again near the top of the hollow. George and Rudy are exhausted, but are determined to get into the action. They pulled themselves toward the latest scene, confident that this time they would get into the action, but again it was not to be. So down into the other side of the hill the battle continued. After 8 or 9 hours they decided that they'd had enough. Their exhausted bodies had lost the desire to join the action. They rested and decided that the bear would win today. At this point they would be lucky to get back to their car before dark. The idea of spending a night in a wet cold mountain forest in the dark wasn't desirable, and they reached their car just before dark. The dog owner was sitting in his truck waiting for his dogs.

The dogs are all tagged with their owner's names and phone numbers and sometimes they don't get back till the next day. The dog owners know each other and their dogs and it being a pretty closed society, they will hold and care for each others dogs. The owners seem to get their joys just listening to the canine chorus, the sound of the hunt sometimes more satisfying than getting the game. They know each of their dogs just by the barks, howls and their yelps. When on the trail, these dogs work hard, but make no mistake; they are well cared for and loved. What George learned about bear hunting on this one and only trip is that playing squash on the level gym floor is no conditioning for chasing dogs and a bear on the move. Up the mountain and sliding down into the hollow is much harder and more exhausting. They were sore for days afterwards. George had difficulty going down the steps at home and at the office with his shins and thighs stiff and sore. Now that he has had some experience with bear hunting he knows that if he ever did it again, he would wait till the dogs really have the bear cornered before he runs to get into the action. That day they never got to see the bear and when the hunter loses, the bear wins the day.

He really admired the team work between the dog owners and their dogs. A symphony with a beautiful canine chorus played in nature's auditorium. A real class act. George decided he wouldn't do it again.

There is a real danger facing the bear and bear hunting.

With the influx of Asian immigrants at that time, the demand for many animal parts soared. For instance the bear's gallbladder is thought to be medicinal in some Asian cultures. This stems from the belief that a bear, once he locates a beehive far up a tree and climbs to the hive, gorges himself on the honey. All that sugar puts him in a stupor and he passes out and falls often from a very high tree. He lies on the ground until the stupor wears off and then gets up and walks away with no apparent injury. They attribute this ability to survive the big fall to the bear's gallbladder. Because of this belief they will pay as high as a thousand dollars for each gallbladder. If the demand remains high the bears will be hunted legally and illegally until extinction. This is a good example of, one man's trash is another man's treasure, and a good economic example of price and demand. Before the Asian demand the bear gallbladder was thrown away. In a few years the selling price went from zero a to hundred dollars and a couple of years later to a thousand dollars. George himself never believed that the gallbladder had any magical healing powers. The one way to stop the hunting of bears for the gallbladder is to debunk the myth that the gallbladder can cure everything or anything.

The Saga of the Old Bull

George was in the exotic food business and as president of

World Safari Inc. he had to travel to the source of the supply for

his products which were considered exotic game at the time, game

such as venison, wild boar, frog, alligator, turtles, rattlesnake, crawfish, pheasant, quail and quail eggs. Anything that crawled slithered or hid under rocks. In this instance George and Pappy went to South Dakota to meet with a small slaughterhouse owner who would be able to supply them with buffalo meat, and a rancher who had lots of buffalo but his main business was raising cattle but was having financial trouble and it had become difficult to keep the bankers happy. The banker was advising him to sell his stock to make his payments. His problem was, he could not sell the cattle and make a profit. He had buffalo to sell but at that time there was no market for buffalo. World Safari wanted to try and introduce buffalo meat to the consumer market in Washington DC and surrounding areas. George decided the best way to do this was by buying the buffalo, have the heads mounted, and take some pictures of the heads to entice the sale of the buffalo meat.

They drove through the ranch, which was huge, to where the cattle were. The rancher explained to them how expensive it was to feed the cattle thru winter and how, during very heavy snows, the only way to get the feed to the cattle was by helicopter. The buffalo on the other hand go right through the winter without any care at all. They managed to keep the snow cleared by bunching together and pushing it away so they can get to the prairie grass on their own. In addition, their big shaggy coats enable them to handle the cold very well. George and Pappy were in a jeep driving to the buffalo heard to shoot the ones they intended to take home. They only had a very small rifle so they needed to get close to the animals but the buffalo were not cooperating. As they got close the buffalo took off and after them they went. Finally, the heard slowed down and they were able to select a large bull and shoot him with a nice clean shot to the neck. It dropped just as it should have but suddenly things changed and we were in the middle of the herd as it began to move in that lumbering rolling style, in a swirling cloud of dust. Suddenly the jeep didn't seem like a very safe place to be. They felt like they were in a stampede in an old John Wayne western. The buffalo went around them and ran some more.

The heard formed family groups of a dozen or so with the adults circling the calves to protect them by keeping them inside the circle. They selected another big patriarchal bull who they thought would make a perfect mount. With the light gun they tried to duplicate the nice neat shot as they did with the first bull, but finding the neck was difficult because the bull was so big and shaggy, forcing them get in real close. With one shot the bull dropped to his knees, but he had only been stunned. The big bull barely got to his feet when a young bull, sensing his weakness began to attack. It wasn't more than 30 seconds from the time the gun was fired to the time the young bull slammed his horns into the injured bull. It was not a head to head test of strength for mating rights as antlered animals do, this was outright murder. The young bull struck the old bull in the loin area which made the old bull spew fluid from his mouth. The force of the impact spun the old bull in a half circle and knocked him to the ground. It got to it's feet again and the young bull struck him again in the loin. 2000 pounds slamming into 2000 pounds! The old bull went down again and struggled to get to its feet like the good warrior he was but Pappy has had enough and let off a quick shot that dropped the old bull for good. The young bull had already started his charge and with horns blowing and lots of shouting we tried to drive him off. He slid to a halt with his nostrils blowing steam right in front of the downed buffalo. He didn't stop his charge because of us, he stopped because the old bull wasn't getting up and he was finished. It was only after young bull was sure the old bull was done in that he became aware of us. He barely gave us a second glance as he ran off to join his family as the new Papa bull with exclusive mating rights The first bull weighed 2000 pounds and the old bull weighed 2009 pounds. We had a local taxidermist mount the heads and send them back to Washington DC where they were placed on display at many hotels whenever they served the wild game and at special wild game festivals. The old bull was even on television.

Years later George sold the mounted head to a local businessman for 1500 dollars and it still hangs on the wall of a restaurant in Alexandria, Virginia.

Was This Stealing?

After a nice day of shooting pheasants in Pennsylvania with a customer, George and Pappy said goodbye to their guests who left in their own car to drive back to the city. They jumped into George's station wagon and started home. On a country road, George spotted a stack of wood that was cut in fireplace lengths and neatly stacked on the side of the road. He asked Pappy, "Whose wood is that, I need firewood at my house." Pappy suggested that they should pull over and load up the wood. George wondered if they should ask some one if it is OK to take some. In his own forceful way Pappy asked," Do you see anyone to ask? Don't be silly George just pull over and get some of the wood." It was a nice stack of wild cherry and George still had reservations about the legality of taking all these goodies but they began to disappear when Pappy pointed out that wild cheery would make your house smell nice but George wondered again, "Who owns this wood." Pappy is becoming impatient with him and pointed out that sometimes utility crews cut down the trees because they were getting too big and would break down the wires, they would shred the smaller pieces and leave the larger pieces for the public. Because Pappy had been a policeman George accepted his explanation and began loading the nice wild cherry logs into the station wagon and filled it to the brim. George dropped Pappy off at his car and proceeded proudly home. He unloaded some wood in his garage and some inside the house next to the warm fireplace. The next morning he proceeded downtown for a meeting with a black activist to discuss plans for setting up a food delivery system to the people who live in the projects in DC. He had the food and the activist had the political access. A good team and a good idea, but it never got off the ground.

On the way downtown George was going to drop off some clothes at the cleaners and get a cup of coffee, when suddenly an 18 inch long snake fell out of the sun visor of the car and onto his right thigh winding up in his cup holder. What a way to start the day! The snake was coiled up nicely in the cup holder and George immediately places his note book over the hole in an attempt to keep him quiet and feeling safe in the dark holder. He was headed to the cleaners but changed his plans and decided to go back home to get a container for the snake until he could decide what to do with him. Riding down the highway he decided to take his pen, lift the notebook and take a peek to make sure the snake was still there and to and try to see his markings. This was the first mistake. He was marked somewhat like his big brother the rattler. Suddenly George hit a bump and the notebook slides off his pen and falls to the floor on the passenger side of the car. This frightens the snake and he shot out onto the floor on the driver's side near the pedals. So here he was in the middle of traffic and afraid of putting his foot on the gas because he might be stepping on the little rascal. He lifted his foot and, of course, the car slowed down with the traffic piling up behind him. He managed to pull over to the side of the road and stop but not before a truck driver raises his fist at him and shouted some obscenities. George decided that things were getting out of hand and he needed help. Being close to home he went there to call the zoo to try and get someone to help. The person at the zoo told him to get the snake out of the car before somebody got killed, as though George didn't already know that. He asked how that might be accomplished and was told to get everything out of the car including the seats. George said that would ruin his car and asks if this is the only way to get rid of the snake. At this time another man got on the phone and explained that he had just gotten back from Africa on a snake catching expedition. He calmly proceeded to tell George what to do. He told him to park the car in the sunniest spot that he could can find, put some gas in an open dish, such as a pie plate and place it in front of the heater as close as possible, roll up the windows tightly, start up the car and turn on the heater. The gasoline fumes would drive the snake out of the car. It was the same procedure he used in Africa where he would take a gasoline soaked rag and stuff it in the snake hole. The fumes would drive the snakes out of the other side of the hole. George thanked him for his good advice, but decided he couldn't do it right away so he decided to attend his meeting first and take care of the snake later.

That was his second mistake. He met Arthur at fast food restaurant. Arthur asked George why he was late and George told him about the snake episode. Immediately Arthur goes crazy and is panic stricken. He said, "Lordy, Lordy, don't ever mention snakes to me. You're making me sick to my stomach.

Just the mention of snakes makes the hairs stand up on my arms."

He then showed George and sure enough the hairs were standing

up. This shortened the meeting very quickly and they walked out

to their cars which were parked side by side. Arthur was carrying

an umbrella and he stood beside me while I opened the driver's

door and things got immediately worse. The snake fell out and

Arthur went into shock. He yelled, "copperhead snake," and fell

against his car door having trouble breathing and sliding to the

ground. George remembered what the man from the zoo said

about getting the snake out of the car before someone got killed.

He got Arthur upright and then remembered that the people at

the zoo told him to bring a snake in, dead or alive, to see if it was

poisonous. Seeing the snake crawling away, he took Arthur's

umbrella and crushed the snake's head killing it. Then he had to

drop the umbrella and grab Arthur who was again sliding to the

ground and yelling, "Copperhead, copperhead!" Even though

Arthur was very small, George had trouble holding him up. He seemed to be fading in and out of consciousness. All the color was gone from his face and George began slapping him gently trying to bring him around. The danger in this situation was that they were in a predominately black neighborhood and George being a big white appeared to be slapping around a small black man. Before Arthur was fully aware of what was going on, George grabbed the dead snake and threw it in his car. He didn't want Arthur to see the snake because that would only put him in shock again. He took the dead snake to the zoo and they said it was not poisonous. They added that there were probably more snakes and they came with the firewood. So George went home and did what they told him the first place. He parked the car in the sun, with a dish of gasoline by the heater, the motor running and the windows closed. He never saw anymore snakes but they might have been burned up in the fireplace.

George later donated that car to a local church in Washington DC. The church used the car for years and they never saw any more snakes. He never discovered who owned that stack wood along side the road. They are usually cut down by the utility crews, but maybe George was stealing them and the snakes were his punishment. If anybody knows whether it's stealing or not please contact him at georgem@metronets.com.

All this happened in a predominately black neighborhood and he believed he was fortunate that no group of brothers passed at that time. It would have been hard to explain why a good sized white man was holding and slapping a nice little blackman.

Rattlesnakes in DC

As president and owner of World Safari, Inc., George was now engaged in supplying exotic foods to upscale restaurants, hotels, and natural food stores. His role in hunting was to find strange items for affluent and international clientele. People from all over the world with different cultures have different ideas of what is good eating. As is sometimes said, one man's trash is another man's treasure. A large and important client was a famous French restaurant named *Dominique's.* Dominique, the owner was French and was cognizant of the appetites of the rich and worldly to which he catered. International dignitaries, Hollywood celebrities, government officials all came to see and be seen and to eat something exotic. Each week he would advertise something different to catch the public's interest and would ask George to supply that item. Since it was his business to do so, George did it. He supplied Dominique with venison, wild boar, alligator, pheasants, quail, wild turkey, squab, antelope, buffalo, duck, quail eggs, wild sheep, and much more. However, these items were becoming mundane and Dominique wanted some thing that would really catch the public's interest, something new. So he asked him to get rattlesnakes. He wasn't sure that George could get them but he assured him that he could, after all that was his business.

He called a friend in Florida, a retired veterinarian who loved to catch snakes. The friend invited him down and told him that he knew exactly where to get some. So George hopped on a plane, and when there, ate some hush puppies and fingerling catfish and was back in Washington the next evening with the snakes. Dominique was excited because he'd advertised the rattlesnakes and they were a huge success. The restaurant was full with orders for rattlesnakes and Dominique requested more which George provided. Again the restaurant was jammed. He needed more fresh rattlesnakes fast, so George contacted some trappers he knew in Pennsylvania, up near the New York border. These are people who trapped in the winter and picked wild herbs during the summer, ginseng and such, dried them, and sold them in the winter to the "sang" man as they called him. They did a little subsistence farming and caught snakes for the hides

and the sport of it.

After working all day, George drove through the night

without sleep to meet them at 8 am to start the hunt. They took

him to the spots where they had caught snakes before. It wasn't

a very productive hunt because snakes are very solitary during

the summer months. Once they leave the den, they lay about on

rocks near the den for a few days soaking up the sun and getting

ready for the hunt. This is the easiest time to gather them up

because until they are warmed up, these cold blooded animals are

slow and much easier to catch but once warmed it's a much more

difficult task, he is much faster and is a solitary hunter. That is

why hunting them in the summer is not too productive. They will

be found one at a time and even those are few and far between.

That day they caught only about 8 snakes and the hunters felt bad

because of the small catch. They therefore decided to let George in on some of their other woodland secrets. After making him swear not to divulge its location, they took him to the north side of the mountain explaining that snakes are found on the south side of the mountain and ginseng on the north. They showed him the growing plants, explaining that it took about seven years for the plant, which had 5 green leaves to a stem and a white blossom when in bloom, to mature. They allowed George to pull two plants from the side of a slanted shady hill, which he took with him when he left the hunters. He iced down the snakes in a refrigerated container in the back of his truck, placed the ginseng plants on the dashboard and started to drive home to Virginia.

He hadn't slept for two nights and after running the mountains all day he was exhausted and looked for a place to spend the night and get something to eat. Hungry and tired, he remembered the ginseng on the dashboard and he decided since it came from clean mountain soil he just shook off the loose dirt and chewed on the root. It tasted fine so he ate the other one. Normally after two days without sleep and all that exercise of roaming the mountains, he would be trying to stay awake, looking for places to stop and get coffee for fear of having an accident but not this time. He had a most enjoyable, relaxed ride and drove all the way home without stopping, from the New York border, through Pennsylvania, Maryland and into Virginia. When he did arrive home he slept for only a few hours and was ready to take on the world, or at least deliver his snakes. This was his only experience with ginseng but he was hooked and ready to commend the virtues of fresh, wild, ginseng. It's great!

When the environmentalists and conservationists heard of *Dominique's* and the snakes they called their Congressmen complaining about using wild endangered creatures for food. The congressman notified the news media that he was going to investigate the restaurant. That evening, eating in the restaurant, was a man from the Department of the Interior (a Snake Department employee) who noticed the rattlers on the menu. He wrote a memo to Dominique stating that the rattlers were on the endangered animal list and should not be sold and therefore should be taken off the menu. Dominique was upset and frustrated. The restaurant was packed and the people were ordering the rattlers. Good promoter that he was, he knew that he had a winner but he couldn't capitalize on it. During the next day or so, the Secretary of the Department of the Interior came into the restaurant. Dominique joined him at his table and asked, "Why can't I sell my snakes?" "Who said you can't?" asks the Secretary. "Your snake man" replies Dominique. The Secretary informed Dominique that he certainly could sell the snakes and sent a letter to Dominique stating that no laws were violated. So Dominique attached the letter to the front door of the restaurant, advertised the rattlesnakes and everybody was satisfied, except the snakes. The Department of the Interior was satisfied that they clarified the issue and that the rattlers were not an endangered species. True, they were declining in numbers but the snake catchers said that there was still an old law on the books in the county where we captured these rattlers that paid a bounty for killing them. The congressmen that promised to investigate Dominique for selling an endangered species were happy. They got free publicity and Dominique was ecstatic because he got thousands of dollars of free advertising and publicity including television exposure and even had camera men visiting his kitchen. Dominique later sold his very successful restaurant and retired and George was proud he was the one who introduced another exotic animal to the eating public. He also learned that government people are human and sometimes make errors and that there are other government people who can and do correct these errors if brought to their attention. He also learned that there are good promoters, like Dominique, who when dealt a lemon, made lemonade or better yet, when handed a snake he made money out of it. He also learned of the benefits of wild ginseng, knows that it grows on the north side of the mountain, and has excellent health benefits. These facts were also known by the recent Asian immigrants who have always known the benefits of this valuable herb. Some have scoured the mountains to gather it in such quantities that some states have classified it as an endangered plant and is not to be plundered. Some State and Federal Government agencies have done wonderful work in bringing back endangered animals. The buffalo is a very good example because they were near extinction at the turn of the century and are now recovering nicely. The buffalo just may be the health meat of the future. They have also saved the wolves, alligators, swans, and ducks and should be commended for their good work.

Trapping is Also Hunting

The equipment in trapping is different and the reason for trapping is also different. Trapping is not food for the table; it is usually for profit and is not camaraderie because it is usually a solitary endeavor. But it must be considered a form of hunting, a low form of hunting, especially when steel leg holding traps are used. Trapping usually means holding an animal by the leg until the trapper inspects his traps and makes his rounds, often times it's a long cruel wait especially with a steel trap biting into the animals leg. While walking his dog in the woods near lake Seneca, New York, George noticed that his dog began to behave oddly, like a male dog when he comes across the scent of a female dog in season. He lifted his leg as though he was staking out his territory he was moving very excitedly toward some invisible attraction. Then suddenly snap. The trap seemed to leap out of the dirt and grab him by the front left leg, the dog in very great pain and was biting at the steel trap rolling over in the dirt, getting to his feet he tries to pull his leg free with no luck. The dog crying in agony and George realized that the dog is out of his mind in pain and that he might get bit unintentionally but it is his dog so he had to forgo the risk and help it. He managed to get the spring that releases the pressure of the trap jaws and free the dog. This was a large shepherd about 90 pounds and strong. The fact that the trap held him you have to wonder what it would do to a smaller dog or animal. It would have probably broken the leg, causing great pain and suffering till the trapper made his rounds. Any one who witnesses an incident such as this would agree that leg traps are cruel and should be made illegal. Checking with the authorities George found that this trap had been set by the state trapper to cut down the fox population and the threat of rabies. There has to be a less cruel method of animal control. Catching animals for mans use is within gods rule [man has dominion over the animals] but He thinks that even God would frown on the use of steel leg traps and everyone must agree that there are other more humane traps.

How Lucky Can I Get?

After introducing fresh frog legs to the upscale food establishments, especially the French restaurants, George was surprised by the strong demand for this product. To supply this demand he thought the place to find this many frogs would be Florida and he inquired about this from some knowledgeable people. He learned that there were Indians who caught frogs near Fort Meyer. So he hopped on a plane and a car and went in search of these frog catchers. He arrived in a little town in Florida and began asking local people if they knew of anyone catching frogs and that he wished to go out at night with them to see their operation and show them how he would like the frogs dressed and packaged for shipment to Washington DC. He offered 100 dollars to accompany a hunter out in the swamps for two hours in the evening to test the idea, however, there were no takers. Normally, in a small rural area this amount of money would bring all sorts of prospects but not this time. He decided to talk to a local policeman he noticed standing near by. Perhaps if he upped the ante he would get better results. He told the officer that he was from Washington, in food business, and would like to get in touch with some one with a small boat to take him out in the swamps at night to catch some frogs and was willing to pay 150 dollars for a two hour tour and that his goal was to set up a frog catching and processing operation. But this approach yielded no takers either.

Disappointed, he called his office and told them of his failure and asked if they could make some inquiries to assist him in finding someone in Florida who might be able to help. He spent the night in the town, went into the local restaurant for breakfast where there were about 12 or 14 people. There was conversation around the diner, normal in a restaurant, but when George sat down the room went quiet. He felt it was strange but he sat down and ordered anyway. It was the quietest restaurant he had ever been in, bordering on eerie. He turned around and all heads went down at the same time. The hair on the back of his neck stood up with the eeriness of the situation, so he decided to get out of that town. He called Sophia at the office in Washington and she informed him that she found a professional frog hunter who was supplying local restaurants with frogs and was eager to expand his market. He had an airboat and was very interested in our project and would take him out in the swamps that very night if I could get to him by 4 pm that evening. George took the "Alligator Alley" he knew was the fastest way to go from the west to the east coast. He met the man who was catching frogs for a living who took him out for gratis and was very much interested in catching and shipping frogs to him and they spent the night in the swamp. They caught and processed the frogs and sent them to Washington.

About three weeks later while getting ready to play his weekly pinochle game George's friend Mack asked of him the name of that town where he went looking for frogs in Florida. He told him and Mack explained that he was lucky he didn't get killed. The Washington Post newspaper had published a story about that town being arrested by the FBI for a drug smuggling operation. The whole town was arrested. Small boats would go out at night and meet a big boat from somewhere off shore. "They were making 150,000 dollars for a night's work and you were offering them 150 dollars for a night," said Mack. George also learned from an expert who made his living from the swamp, how abundant wild life was in the swamp and what a lonely job it was. The only life you'd see or hear was an occasional plane going overhead. With his strong lamp attached to his head and plugged into the magneto of the motor of his airboat, the hunter seeks his prey. The eyes that reflect back as pearls are the frogs sitting on the lily pads. The hunter must gauge the distance, slow down the boat, and steer it in close enough to spear the frog or gig it with a barbless prong which is attached to a plastic tube about six feet long. He then slides the frog off the prongs into a funnel and then into a perforated bag which rests on the floor beneath his seat. He must be very dexterous and accurate to make it pay. That strong light brings out lots of things you would not ordinarily see, such as, the fire red eyes of the gators that look like burning coals. Some gators are as long as the air boat and when you go too close to some small trees you can hear plunk, plunk, these are the snakes that you shook or scared out of the trees. When you step on a small island, and it moves, you know that this is a floating island. If you see a swamp rabbit it will have a collar of worms that looks like a necklace which is normal for a swamp rabbit. There are marsh hens, or as George calls them swamp chickens, raccoons, deer, and wild pigs. There are lots of wild creatures and the lone frogger. He must also be a good air boat mechanic because there are no repair shops nearby.

This swamp hunter is the same alligator hunter who was to be featured on the T.V. show *60 Minutes* when alligators were taken off the endangered list. He invited George to be in one of the boats as a representative of the exotic food industry, to explain how the gator meat would be introduced to the public, and how it would enter the food distribution system. Unfortunately, George was out of town and was unable to meet the time dead line. "Hell, I never even got to see the show," he commented.

Hunting Animals for Research

Since he was involved in hunting and processing animals it was a natural progression that he began to supply animals and animal parts for research facilities such as Walter Reed, N.I.H, .Georgetown University, Micro Biological etc.   One particular request for animal parts for research would have an impact personally on him. The request was for a heart and arteries of a calf around 200 pounds within 2 hours of death, which actually was no problem. They evidently micron the valves to make new ones because the next request was for a 200 pound live calf in which to insert the valves. About 6 months later the researchers called him to pick up the calf which was no longer a calf but weighed about a thousand pounds and had now outgrown his space, so the experiment was a success. He took the cow to a farm in Centerville, Virginia where it lived happily to a ripe old age.

This makes one reflect on the importance of animals to medical research. I don't believe there is a single person in this country that has not been touched by the benefits of animals used for research. While preparing for his own bypass operation, George began to count the number of friends and family who had the same procedure. Three of his brothers did, as well as his neighbor and pinochle partner. All were successful and are enjoying a better, healthier and longer life. Here George was on the operating table waiting in full confidence that his operation would be successful because the doctor who was to operate on him was familiar with the researcher who had perfected the operation on the calf he had provided. He felt good knowing that he might have had a little part in improving the health of many. Many animal rights activists object to the use of animals for research but you can rest assured that their family and friends have benefited from this research. But like the activist, George is against unnecessary pain or abuse to research animals.

Another instance when he had personally benefited from the research animal parts he provided was when he was undergoing a cataract procedure. He noticed on the wall of his doctor's office a certificate of accreditation from a school to which he had been supplying animal eyeballs so the students could learn how to perform surgery and to learn how the eye operates. They evidently learned well because his cataract surgery was a success.

148

Monkey Business

Most animal parts for research are taken from domestic animals that were being prepared for human consumption by a licensed abattoir. However, some of the more exotic animals, such as monkeys, had to be brought in from other countries. This proved to be difficult at times because of the language barriers. George had an excellent reputation for supplying hard to get items for research which resulted in a request to supply 12 pregnant rhesus monkeys. No one had been able to breed rhesus monkeys in captivity so they would have to be imported from a country where they are indigenous and which would require him to go to and oversee the capture. However, the time limit placed on the request required that he trust a Pakistani with whom he had done business in the past. His name was Mujibulla. George later found out that the animals would be part of the space race with the Russians who at the time had a dog in space. So he called Mujibulla and asked if he could supply the pregnant monkeys. He told George that he could and that he should send the money. George felt this was too easy but he went along with it because of the urgency of the client. The monkeys arrived at Dulles International Airport and he and his crew raced out to accept the delivery and get them to the client.

The monkeys were in twelve separate cages. The two man crew carried the cages on their shoulders using two poles from which the cages were hung. George was wearing a safari jacket and it looked as though they had just come from the jungle. Inside was the client and his cohorts, dressed in nice white laboratory coats. He knew that this wasn't going to be a normal delivery but he handed his invoice to the man who seemed to be in charge, for him to sign. George was eager to be reimbursed because of the expense incurred. The transaction was great, having flown the monkeys halfway around the world and having paid Mujibulla in advance with no guarantee of the results. So he presented

his invoices and asked that they be signed. The man said that

he must check to see if the monkeys were indeed pregnant. He

called to an attendant to get one of the monkeys. It took two

to handle the animal. One, wearing steel mesh gloves reached

inside one of the cages and extracted a monkey which was

biting the glove without stop. With his other hand he grabbed

the monkey by the back of the neck and held it down as she

continued to bite the glove. This caused her to raises her rump

which allowed the other attendant to perform the procedure to

determine if she was pregnant. With a big production the main

examiner puts out his hand and yelled, "glove," and another

attendant snaps a rubber glove on his hand. Then he yelled,

"oil," and a different attendant puts oil on his finger. The main

examiner inserts his middle finger in the monkey. And after a

bit he said, "not pregnant, put the monkey on the other side of the room." This revelation got George's attention and he quickly calculated that he would still make out OK if the others were all pregnant. The examiner called for monkey number 2 and goes through the same procedure, "Glove", "oil", and again his says, "not pregnant, put the monkey on the other side of the room." George quickly calculated mentally that the profit would be less but he would still be OK. Then again with monkey number 3 and again, "Glove", "oil", and again his says, "not pregnant, put the monkey on the other side of the room." By this time George determined that he would be lucky to break even. When they got to the 9th monkey he realized that something was wrong because none had been pregnant thus far. Either the examiner was wrong or Mujibulla made an error. There was no way to check with Mujibulla at this time so he asked the examiner if he was sure that the monkeys were not pregnant He said, "we ordered pregnant Rhesus monkeys and these are absolutely not pregnant."

Concerned George decides to check for himself. He pushed the examiner aside and says, "glove", "oil", "hold that monkey", and proceeded to check, not sure what he is feeling for so he asks the examiner. The examiner tells him that he will feel a lump the size of a walnut if the monkey is pregnant but there was nothing. He checked the rest of the monkeys and realized that Mujibulla was the culprit. He must have captured a bunch of monkeys and selected the fattest ones thinking they were pregnant. He more than likely did not have the expertise to determine if the monkeys were pregnant.

George learned that Mujibulla was a good businessman. He asked for the money in advance and was paid for monkeys that were not pregnant. George also learned how to palpate a monkey which his employees found humorous and teased him about it.. They made jokes like, "the monkey stopped snarling and began to smile and blow kisses at him." George on the other hand could only see his profit dwindling, however, the lab was fair and paid

him the price for regular, non-pregnant, monkeys. He felt bad

that he failed to deliver a good product when his country needed

it in a hurry, but he tried his best.

How Not To Do It

Just as early man learned it was more economical to farm and contain the animals (ranches) rather than going forth every day to capture his prey. George with his exotic food and his biological research businesses growing he decides to do the same. He would farm as much as possible the birds fishes, frogs were most often in demand. Time was often of the essence and supply was often short. On two lakes he stocks bass, catfish and sunfish, chickens that laid green eggs, geese, ducks and frogs, yes frogs. The frogs were always in demand for research and upscale restaurants that thirsted for fresh frog legs. They were and still are in great demand. Flying to Florida to increase supply was too expensive and time consuming. So seeing an add in a sport magazine advertising giant 5 pound frogs, George decided to fly them in and introduced them into the new lakes, and this was a poor idea since we had already stocked the lake with fish , duck and geese. The frogs were flown in and released into the lake in late summer .All winter he waited and waited and sure enough spring came and the shallow end of the lake was filled with thousands and thousands of eggs, (frog eggs.) .George is feeling smug and proud and sees great profit and future riches before his very eyes. He saw thousands and thousands of eggs turning into thousands of frogs and these turning into thousands of dollars. At that time he didn't realize how true the old saying was (don't count your chickens before they are hatched.) Each weekend he would drive down to see how his treasure was growing and he could see the tadpoles inside the eggs getting larger and larger each week. He was sure they would hatch by the next weekend. With great anticipation he made the trip hoping to see the glorious hatch. Arriving at the lake, he is treated to a great surprise, instead of a glorious event it was a great catastrophe. The surface of the water was alive with ducks and geese in an eating frenzy. Just imagine hundreds of ducks and geese eating his potential profits.

Those little tadpoles had no chance. The ducks and geese got

them as soon as they hatched and even before they hatched. Any

that had hatched and had escaped the birds had to face the bass

and other fishes that were waiting for them as they came out of

the shallows and into deeper water. This eating frenzy by the

ducks, created an additional set back for this endeavor. While

the ducks were eating the tadpoles, their nests with their own

eggs were left unguarded. The ever clever, opportunistic crows

were attacking the duck eggs in the unguarded duck nests. They

would poke a hole in the egg and pull out the unborn duckling

and devour it or carry it to its own young. Farming frogs can be

profitable, but remember everything and everybody loves frogs.

Bird's animals' turtles fish snakes and of course man etc. They

must be protected to make it profitable. I would like to try this

again, I know it would work. If anybody has any interest, contact me.　Lesson learned: don't count your chickens or your frogs

before they are hatched.

George Becomes the Prey

While hunting animals for profit and research and enjoying financial success, George was not aware that he and his company World Safari Incorporated were being hunted for profit by a smarter, smoother hunter. This hunter didn't use a gun, he used a pen and someone else's checkbook, in this instance, World Safari's. He is known as "the trusted accountant." By the time the trusted accountant was snared in March of 1997 he had embezzled 687,000 dollars. The hunter was charged and he pled guilty to the crime of grand larceny in the circuit court of Arlington County, Virginia, and on July 16, 1997 he made partial restitution to World Safari but the prey was deeply injured financially by this smooth trusted hunter/embezzler.

The lesson learned is that there is always a smarter hunter nearby. They don't always use a gun, sometimes it's just a pen.

Any man reading this and is starting his own business beware of

this hunter. Hear ye! Hear ye! You have been warned.

The Future Role of the Hunter of Old

The hunter of old and the maker of the man-made rule that postulates that men are the providers and women are the child-bearers and home makers has lasted for a million years but, is being changed right now. When humans became more efficient and changed from a hunter-gatherer society to a farming-animal containment society, man no longer had to hunt the animals to provide for his family. The animals were on his farm or ranch and easily accessible. He learned that it was more economical to get a job and earn some money to go to the market and buy his meat and bring to the table. Even though they changed his name from hunter to plumber, carpenter, electrician, doctor, or lawyer he was still the hunter of old and the primary provider and protector of the family. With the start of World War II, with so many men away from home fighting, women entered the work force in record numbers. They did jobs that the men had been doing to earn money to provide for the family. When the war ended there was a brief period in which the men (hunters of old) resumed their leadership role but, it didn't last long.

Another key in bringing about change in gender roles was the invention of the pill. The pill, or oral female contraceptive, helped to free women from the almost constant role of child bearing and the responsibility of insuring the survival of the human race. Women no longer had to stay at home, barefoot and pregnant, at the whim of the dominant male. Women could now have children, when and if she wanted or delay them until a later more convenient time. She was now free from that man-made-rule that kept her in bondage for a million years. "I have the big muscles I will be the hunter-provider and since you are built for child bearing you will stay at home." Women were now primed to challenge the male for the role of hunter and provider. Hail to the new and better hunter and provider, and she is better equipped in this society to fulfill the role because big muscles are no longer necessary for the survival of the human race. Women can fly a plane, practice law, become doctors and run computers. They can do everything a man can do, even launch missiles. Big muscles and physical strength are not needed in this society. Brains and the desire to use them now rule over brawn. Women have brains and in this society it is the female who has the greatest desire to achieve. The proof of this is the fact that 60 percent of the students entering college are female who also have the best grades. Women are striving and the males seem to be coasting along. As far as the ability to handle stress, women are much better. Insurance statistics show that women outlive men by far and they say that women control 85 percent of the wealth in the US because of inheritance and the collection of life insurance. This may have been the only way women amassed wealth in the past but it is not the only way today. Women can do every thing the male can do and perhaps do it better. They can also do some things a man can't such as child bearing and breast-feeding. Though Y2K was not the end of the world as some "gloom sayers" predicted, it might have been the end of the role of the male hunter and the rise of the new and better female hunter. Once women attained the right to vote it only took 70 years to achieve equality and will only take another decade to achieve dominance. Imagine, if you will, a female dominated society. Because women already control most of the wealth in the US and outnumber males, it will be very easy for women to outvote the men. Already there are many female politicians and it is not unlikely that there could be a female president by 2008 if not sooner. Women are not completely aware of the opportunity that is available to them but with the continued education, financial wealth and political powers it is only a matter of time before the roles will be reversed. It is only a matter of time before the man-made-rule of male dominance over women will be overturned and a new woman-made-rule put in its place. This rule will state that women are stronger, have better educational credentials; a greater desire to use the brain and a better ability to handle stress therefore will be the primary provider for the family and you, the male will stay home and take care of the domestic duties. Men, beware once female dominance is achieved, your life will be different. You will be relegated to the menial jobs such as clerks, cleaners and cooks. You will be treated just as men have treated women for the last million years. The best looking ones will be kept as geisha boys or misteresses as women were. This is already evident with wealthy women who have their "boy toys" and many more women are marrying younger men. Male society as we know it is changing fast. The hunter of old is endangered. What can men do? Not much, they have had it too easy for too long. The only suggestion is to find an area that you can dominate, if not try to find an area you can at least be equal in.

Don't try to hide behind foolish statements such as; women will

always need us to father their children and other myths of that

sort. With the miracle of modern science, especially the advances

being made in human reproduction technology such as artificial

insemination, test tube fertilization, and cloning, they don't need

a man, just a few cells. A woman produces one egg at a time

to be fertilized and the male ejaculation produces thousands of

sperm cells with each event and it only takes one sperm to do

the job. Sperm can be frozen and stored for use at a later date.

The theoretical and mathematical possibilities are astronomical.

There are thousands of sperm in each male ejaculation and there

can be thousands of such ejaculations in a male's life span. This

makes it conceivable that it would only take a couple of men to

populate a whole nation. Forget the idea that men will always

be needed for the sex, with all the new advances being made in the pharmaceutical department is it really so inconceivable that a pill could be invented that will give the same result while you sleep, and what about electric devices? Men, the writing is on the wall, the die is cast, so get out and go to work on the problem. You need help. Do as all the minorities have done in the past, affirmative action will help, ask for it from colleges which have trouble getting enough males into academia, ask for and insist on academic allowances for males. Ask for government financial aid to help with the cost of college. You will soon be earning less than your female counterparts or should I say your superiors. Mainly be aware of the change that is coming fast. I am making no judgment about this coming female dominated society I am merely pointing out that fast change is here and now. If I had to make a judgment about a female society, I would probably say give it a fair chance. Men have led mankind for a million years and we haven't been able to solve many of the world's problems such as hunger, famine and war. I'd be willing to give the females a try at it. Because women bear and nurture the children they might not be so eager to send their sons to war to die on the battlefield and just maybe eliminate war as a way of settling our differences. What about the long range future of the male hunter and provider? The future is dismal. His big muscles are of little use in the new female dominated society and his role of importance will diminish because he will be less educated and earn less money. His lower earnings and stature will also lessen his political power. Man eventually may go the way of the dinosaur and become extinct. Why? Because there will be no need for him. Remember that old man made rule that established male dominance? I have the big muscles so I will be the hunter and I will go forth and provide and you are plainly built for bearing and nurturing of children and you will stay home and do just that. This unwritten rule has lasted for 1 million years. Now with the reversal of roles the female is better prepared to go forth and be the hunter and provider. And she is going to do just that and you, poor male, will stay home for a little while but in the long run, because you can't even bear and nurture children, there will be no need for you.

I am the new hunter and provider because

I am a stronger

Better educated

Have more money

And have more political power

I will go forth and be the hunter provider and you will stay home to care for the children and the home

This is all right for now, but ----

Since you can't bear children your future is very dim. In the long term there will be no need for your and your muscles. Like the dinosaurs you are headed for extinction..

What about the Modern Sport Hunter

What is the modern recreational hunter doing while non-hunters are making decisions concerning his interests? Nothing! He is standing by doing nothing while non-hunters are making decisions that he should have a voice in making. For example, non-hunters who oppose hunting with a gun say they oppose killing. But they think it is perfectly correct to poison 5000 crows at one feeding because there cars get dirty when they are park under the trees where the crows roost at night. They also complain that the crows make too much noise. These are the same people that are anti-hunting and anti-guns but they don't mind murdering thousands of crows silently because they are an inconvenience. Who knows what kind of effects this form of killing has on the environment such as the untold number of animal ,birds, insects and worms that feed off the sick and dying birds and what are the effects if the poisons get washed into the sewers and creeks and then into the bay and eventually into the ocean. The fish will ingest these poisons and man will eat the fish and slowly and silently these poisons will sicken and kill humans. Although God gave man dominion over the animals I think even God would shudder at the horrible, sickening way we have resorted to killing the crows and poisoning the environment. The hunters could solve the problem with much less damage to the environment by having a crow shoot. They could select a spot a little distant from the population in an open field and set up a decoy or a recording with a crow battle cry to lure the crows. Crows from miles around that hear the battle cry will come from miles away to join in the fray. Then shooters can shoot till their gun gets hot. The crow population would get cut down immediately with out much damage to other animals and the environment. Hunters you know how to solve these problems if you don't speak up these uninformed bureaucrats will destroy all of God's creatures and your quality of life. Doesn't any one

remember DDT? DDT was a pesticide that almost wiped out the

Eagle, our national bird. The Canadian goose is another problem

that is trying to be solved by non-hunters. There are too many

resident geese around our school grounds, our golf courses and

our airports. This is a looming problem because a flock of geese

can bring down a plane if the plane was to fly into the geese at the

airport. They chase the geese from the airport with loud noises

and other schemes that only chase the geese away temporally.

The geese keep coming back in increasing numbers. So why

don't you hunters solve the problem? Goose hunters know the

drill. Feed the geese in an area off to the side some where, put

out a few decoys, play a tape recording of feeding geese and let

the hunters do their job. As I said before there is something final

about a shotgun and birds. Then the fresh meat can be taken to a

dressing plant and feed them to the poor and homeless. All this is within Gods plan and our environment is protected from poison.

Hunters speak up now or all hunting will soon be done with a can

of poison. Another concern is the city deer. They are all over the

place. Why? No hunting allowed inside city limits, that's why,

the population of mountain or rural deer remains constant and

urban or city deer are rapidly increasing in numbers. The hunters

harvest the deer in rural areas, where as city deer are protected

by laws that forbid harvesting them, which is against Gods law.

(Man has dominion over the animals) These shortsighted laws

are giving animals rule over man and can not last. Therefore

the urban deer are multiplying rapidly with no predators to keep

their numbers down. Deer in the city are a hazard to humans

as well as to themselves because of automobile collisions.

Sometimes it's not only the deer that gets hurt; there are an

alarming number of accidents involving deer. If not controlled

we will soon have to have grids put on auto bumpers to protect deer from coming thru the windshield which is what they had

to do in New Zealand. Either that or don't drive at night. Deer

like all animals respond to food and the opportunity to mate with

food and or a salt lick they can be lured to a quiet area and killed

by hunters. The deer can be fed to the poor and homeless. Again

this is all with in Gods law   that man has dominion over the

animals. They are his to use and control. If the hunters don't

speak to the uninformed non-hunting civic leaders will give the

animals dominion over man. Modern hunters rise up and are

heard because you are endangered too. In the Washington Post

article that appeared the news Oct. 21, 2003 was a story about a

dear that had ran through a window of the Fairfax Courthouse,

shattering the window and ran through the lobby. The deer was

assaulting the very institution that gave him absolute protection

from the hunter's guns. The bureaucratic headquarters that put

forth the no hunting laws, the same laws that allow the deer to pillage private residential property and collide with autos causing injuries and damage to private citizens had now caused damage on the public fortress. Perhaps now they will see the light and call in the hunters who can solve the problem of over-population. . This deer should have been shot and fed to the poor and needy before he became a pest and a danger to humans. Unless the modern recreational hunter speaks up his future will be very dim. More laws will be passed limiting the area in which he can hunt and more gun restrictions will be enforced. Yes, modern hunter you are endangered, you are the prey. A few more laws and a can of poison can wipe out you and your guns.

Purpose of this Book

To alert the hunter of old, that great male provider and protector of the family, that he is endangered and is on the way down and out and he is being replaced by a better female hunter.

To alert the modern sport hunter that he too is endangered.

He is being voted out by ridiculous laws that say no hunting

allowed which really means no guns allowed, and that poisons

and foolish laws will replace him and his gun as a weapon of

choice to control the animals.

Jokes Told by Hunters

Joe and Sam were both about 85 years of age and were discussing dying and a possibility of life after death, and reincarnation. They decide whichever one dies first he would try to contact the one living and tell him what it's like in the next life. Joe dies, and sometimes later Sammy is awakened by a voice calling, Sammy, Sammy wake up it's your friend Joe. Sammy says tell me Joe what are you, where are you and what are you doing? Joe says "I wake up very early every morning and make love, 10AM I make love again, noon I make love again, same thing all day and all night." Sammy all excited says "I know what you are and where you are. You must be a young man and you are in heaven "Joe replies "I'm a rabbit and I am in Montana."

Papa dog takes puppy son to town to teach him the facts of life. Coming to a garbage can, he overturns it and says "eat" and they pick up a few scraps and continue on their way. They come across a female in heat and papa mounts her and tells the son to do the same, which he does. They continue on their walk and come upon a fire hydrant; papa lifts his leg and tells the son to do the same, which he does. On the walk home papa asked "what did you learn today son?" Son says "I learned when we turned over the garbage can and got some good things to eat, that was good". I learned when we mounted the female in heat that was good. What I don't understand why we piddled on the fire hydrant. Papa says "Son if you can't eat it, if you can't make love to it just piddle on it."

Out in the dessert an Arab is walking his post with his dog guarding his side of the border with Israel, and an Israeli is walking with his dog guarding his side of the border. They have been out there a number of days just the two of them with their dogs and they are bored. Passing each other, they get to talking as bored men will do. The Arab says that's an ugly little dog you have there, big head no tail and all yellow. The Israeli says "he's not as big as your dog, but he is a real bad fighting dog." Then they agree. Since we will never be able to decide which side will win the war, why don't we let our dogs fight. We will make believe that the dog who wins his side will win the war. The Israeli says "no because this ugly yellow dog with the big head and no tail is a terrible fighting machine and your dog would not have a chance." The Arab insists that they let the dogs fight and they do. With one bite the yellow dog bites the big dog right in half and with one gulp he swallows one half and with another gulp he swallows the other half. The Arab says "man you are right that is some kind of fighting dog. What kind is he?" The Israeli replies "before we cut off his tail and painted him yellow he was a crocodile."

Boy and girl rabbits eating carrots in Mr. McGregor's garden at night. Boy rabbit pulls out a carrot and says "ugh!" this carrot tastes pithy. The girl rabbit says "it should taste pithy because I just pith on it."

Did you hear about the man who got herpes on his eye lid?

He was looking for love in the wrong places.

Did you hear about the man who lost his testicles in an accident and wants to get married, but he is afraid that he won't be able to perform his marriage duties. He goes to his Doctor and tells him his trouble. Dr. says "don't worry we can take care of it. We are making great stride in medicine today. We are transplanting hearts, livers etc. Man and the apes are very closely linked on the evolutionary scale. We will get you some monkey testicles and nobody will know and you will be just fine." The operation is scheduled and is very successful. He gets married and nine months later has a baby (home delivery). The doctor, who did the monkey testicle operation, calls up his patient to congratulate him. "I heard the good news, is it a boy or girl?" His ex-patient says "how in hell can we tell? We can't get him down from the chandelier."

What about the Old Hunter

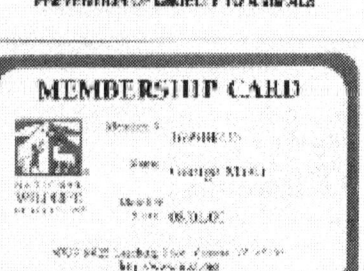

**Old Hunters never die-they
Just become old
conservationists**

About The Author

Personal goal of author – to remind public: Hunting is a God given right – (animal control). Man has dominion over the animals, birds, fishes – He can hunt + eat them – work them – tame and pet them and yes – even use them for research – This is God's Law and cannot be changed. Foolish man made laws that allow deer-geese-crows-etc to multiply unchecked are against his laws – Man rules the animals not animals ruling our cities – etc. Anti gun laws, no hunting allowed – and poisons are poor attempts for animal control – Let the hunters do their work.

www.ingramcontent.com/pod-product-compliance
Lightning Source LLC
Chambersburg PA
CBHW022246290526
45785CB00015B/341